"LIFE WAS MEANT TO BE LIVED"

"LIFE WAS MEANT TO BE LIVED"

A Centenary Portrait of

ELEANOR ROOSEVELT

JOSEPH P. LASH

W·W·NORTON & COMPANY

New York   *London*

Copyright © 1984 by Joseph P. Lash

All rights reserved
Published simultaneously in Canada by Stoddart, a subsidiary of
General Publishing Co. Ltd, Don Mills, Ontario
Printed in the United States of America

The text of this book is composed in Baskerville, with display type set in
Goudy Old Style and Goudy Bold. Composition by Vail-Ballou Press, Inc.
Manufacturing by The Murray Printing Company.
Book design by Christine Aulicino

FIRST EDITION

Library of Congress Cataloging in Publication Data
Lash, Joseph P., 1909–
"Life was meant to be lived."

1. Roosevelt, Eleanor, 1884–1962.   2. Roosevelt,
Franklin D. (Franklin Delano), 1882–1945.   3. Presidents
—United States—Wives—Biography.   I. Title.
E807.1.R48L367   1984   973.917′092′4 [B]   84–1589

ISBN 0-393-01877-6

W. W. Norton & Company, Inc., 500 Fifth Avenue, New York, N.Y. 10110
W. W. Norton & Company Ltd., 37 Great Russell Street, London WC1B 3NU

1 2 3 4 5 6 7 8 9 0

CONTENTS

FOREWORD

IT IS FITTING that W. W. Norton & Company should have asked my friend Joe Lash to do this centenary portrait of my mother.

From the time of her first association with him in the late thirties she valued his friendship and he came to know her as well as anyone outside of her immediate family. He and his wife, Trude, became part of the extended household that my father and my mother, especially, gathered around themselves. There were few family confidences to which they were not privy. And what mother did not tell Joe careful scholarship has enabled him to fill in here, as in his other remarkable volumes about my mother's life.

FRANKLIN D. ROOSEVELT, JR.

PREFACE

"A GREAT MAN lays upon posterity the duty of understanding him," wrote John Buchan in his magisterial life of Oliver Cromwell. There is rich reward in the study of Eleanor Roosevelt. A British social critic observed that "in her personal struggle for self-awareness she was the greatest of the Roosevelts." The remarkable store of self-documentation that she left us in her letters and journals shows us a woman of endless paradox and not infrequent self-contradictions. That is the way most lives are when they rise to the level of self-knowledge. But the path of self-discovery that Eleanor Roosevelt walked was especially important for the growth and enrichment that it made possible in her life.

It was George Brockway's idea that I write this centenary portrait. The manuscript was read and improved by the additional comments of Trude Lash, Merloyd Lawrence, and Evan Thomas.

ACKNOWLEDGMENTS

Following are the sources of black and white photographs that appear in the book: the Franklin D. Roosevelt Library, pages 4, 5, 7, 8 (top two), 11, 12, 14, 16, 17, 19, 22, 24 (bottom two), 25, 26, 46 (left), 64, 93 (bottom), 104, 107, 111, 113 (bottom), 121 (top), 130, 145, 166 (top), 170 (bottom), 175, 185, 190, 197; Mrs. Von Schaeffer-Bernstein, pages 8 (bottom) and 21; Pach Bros., page 13; The Bettman Archive, Inc., pages 18 (top), 36, 45, and 72; Wide World Photos, pages 46, 50 (top), 58 (right), 60, 61, 74 (top), 127 (bottom), and 163; United Press International, pages 50 (bottom), 71, 74 (bottom), 93 (top right), 98, 99, 102, 118, 120 (top), 121 (bottom), 127 (top), 128, 138, 148 (bottom), and 172; the *New York Daily News*, page 56; Martin Vos, page 59; Bachrach, Inc., page 94; Jackie Martin, page 103; Thomas McAvoy, page 106; Cecil Beaton/Camera Press, page 108; Planet News Ltd, page 109 (top); Photographic News Agencies, page 109 (bottom); *Look* magazine, pages 113 (top), 192 (bottom), and 193 (top); Tom Hollyman, page 120 (bottom); Keystone Press Agency, Inc., page 129; the United Nations, pages 139 and 148 (top); Harry Rubenstein, page 140; Edna P. Gurewitsch, page 150 (photo by Maureen Corr) and pages 180, 181, 186 (bottom), 192 (top), 193 (bottom), and 198 (photos by Dr. A. David Gurewitsch); Press Information Bureau, Government of India, pages 166 (bottom) and 167 (top); Leo Rosenthal, pages 167 (bottom) and 191; the American Association for the United Nations (cartoon by Herblock), page 173; Tilyou Studio, page 176; F. Schlesinger, page 182; Jan Studio, page 186 (top); and Field Enterprises, page 196 (bottom).

The color photographs following page 86 are from the following sources: the Franklin D. Roosevelt Library, plates 1, 4, and 11; *Vogue,* Copyright © 1940 (renewed 1968) by The Condé Nast Publications Inc., plate 2; United Press International, plate 3; Yousuf Karsh, plate 5; Henry Kaufman, plate 6; Edna P. Gurewitsch, plates 7, 8, 9, 10, 13, and 14 (photos by Dr. A. David Gurewitsch); and Howard Sochurek, plate 12.

"LIFE WAS MEANT TO BE LIVED"

1

FROM THE BEGINNING

As time passes, the perspective of what a man has lived by is probably more important than the actual things he did, because new situations necessitate new answers and one cannot apply the same theories or exact methods. The background of a man's thinking and acting is at all times a living thing.

—ELEANOR ROOSEVELT TO JOHN G. WINANT

ELEANOR ROOSEVELT WROTE no laws and appointed no high officials, yet the self-knowledge and profound humility that invested her regard for every human being has made the story of her life a morality play that brightens the American memory. "There is no human being," wrote Eleanor Roosevelt in one of her last books, "from whom we cannot learn something if we are interested enough to dig deep." This basic sense of kinship with which she approached the world dictated her vocation of helpfulness. The honesty with which she told us of the long path she traveled to free herself of fear and prejudice and become an independent person has placed her in that special pantheon reserved for shapers of the human spirit. "At this critical point," wrote a journalist about women's long struggle to free themselves from "their husband's dutiful shadows . . . Eleanor Roosevelt appeared on the American scene, and began being herself, out in the open where folks could see the process."

"It is said that famous men are usually the product of an unhappy childhood," wrote Winston Churchill about John Churchill, the first Duke of Marlborough. "The stern compression of circumstance, the

Eleanor's mother and father and her great-grandmother, Elizabeth Livingston Ludlow.

spur of slights and taunts in early years are needed to evoke that ruthless fixity of purpose and tenacious mother-wit without which great actions are seldom accomplished." His words, about an unhappy childhood shaping the greatness of later years, were applicable to Eleanor Roosevelt.

Her autobiography described a child's plainness. She was the only Hall girl not likely to be a belle. That puzzled her brilliant looking, society-minded mother, whose "Come in, Granny" Eleanor remembered all her life, for the nickname made her ashamed. Perhaps it was the secret wound that drove her to excel in other fields. Even as a young girl attending the fashionable Roser classes, she wrote presciently that mediocre looks in a woman might be offset by her "truth and loyalty." The composition went on to affirm that the ability to do good to all who came near her was a manifestation of "one of the greatest gifts that God has given men, the power of friendship. . . ." Thus, in a flash she laid out the course of conduct that she followed all her life.

An unhappy childhood stamped her psyche with a fear of abandonment that not only haunted her but may also have engendered her "hyperactivity"—the word used about Churchill but equally applicable to her—although her stamina and vitality seem innate rather than family-bred qualities.

Her mother died when Eleanor was eight, but even more desolating was the death of her father, Elliott, when she was ten. He was handsome and hapless, the protector in their early years of his older brother, Theodore, who, however, soon bested him in life's little competitions. Theodore went on to high public office while he, afflicted with brain disease, alcoholism, and drug addiction, died young, exiled from his family. He always remained the subject of the passionate longings of Eleanor's dreams. After her mother's death her father, dressed in black, had been allowed to come to see her at Grandma Hall's. "It was always he and I," she wrote.

> . . . There started that day a feeling which never left—that he and I were very close together, and some day would have a life of our own together.
>
> Some day I would make a home for him again; we would travel together and do many things which he painted as interesting and pleasant, to be looked forward to in the future together.
>
> Somehow it was always he and I. I did not understand whether my brothers were to be our children or whether

TOP: *Edward H. Ludlow, Eleanor's great-grandfather and New York City's leading realtor after the Civil War.* BOTTOM: *The first Theodore Roosevelt: a big, powerful man with a "troubled conscience."*

he felt that they would be at school and college and later independent.

Two years later he, too, was dead, and a fear of loneliness and abandonment became ruling emotions in her life.

She concealed such fears and longings that both shaped her approach to reality and prepared the way for deep disappointments in her relationships with others, especially men. "Dearest Boy," she sometimes started letters to the man she loved. That was the caressing salutation used by one of her father's southern aunts in writing to him. Eleanor's use of it in writing to Franklin during their courtship vibrated with the image of her beloved father. Her memory of him strengthened her efforts to live up to his expectations of her. He had been a man of tender chivalry, and she wanted her man to behave similarly. But men did not live up to such ideals, including the wish that they remain permanently and exclusively hers. And somewhere, too, she carried the forbidden knowledge of her father's weaknesses—his bouts of drunkenness, use of drugs, and philandering. Life and the veiled memories of her father's frailties in time made her more tolerant of weaknesses in others.

All these traits were there at the outset of this child of old New York and the Hudson River aristocracy, and her life became an American legend because of the way she responded to the vicissitudes of the twentieth century.

The Civil War still reverberated when she was born. Great-uncles related to her grandmother, the Georgia-born Mittie Bulloch, had commanded a Confederate privateer and were obliged after 1865 to live abroad. Mittie and her sister often told their children how as girls in Georgia they had had their own slaves who had slept at the foot of their beds. Eleanor's mother was descended from the Livingstons. "Three of your ancestors," she reminded her grandchildren on the Fourth of July, when often she had one of her sons read the Declaration of Independence aloud at the poolside cottage at Hyde Park, "were among the signatories. Do you know which?" And then there were the Roosevelts, the first of whom had arrived in New Amsterdam from Holland in the 1640s, to whom she was related by descent (on her father's side) and by marriage.

She took pride in the contributions her family had made to the building of America, and though she was brought up to believe women shared in these achievements only as daughter, wife, or mother, even within such circumscribed limits she welcomed the possibility of women making their mark on the times. She was the favorite niece

Eleanor (right) with her father and two brothers, Hall (on his father's lap) and Elliott.

Eleanor and Hall.

Eleanor and her father in Hempstead, Long Island, where he had built a house.

FAR LEFT: *After her parents' deaths Eleanor lived with her grand-mother, Mrs. Hall, at Tivoli, over-looking the Hudson. "I was fond of horses but not of long stockings and high shoes."* LEFT: *Again at Tivoli. At the reins is her Aunt Maude, youngest of the beautiful Hall sisters.*

At fifteen she was sent to Allenswood, a finishing school on the outskirts of London run by Mlle Souvestre, the remarkable daughter of a French philosophe.

of Aunty Bye, Mrs. Sheffield Cowles, her father's older sister, of whom another niece, Theodore Roosevelt's daughter Alice, tart, witty, and aggressive, said, "If Aunty Bye had been a man she would have been president." Eleanor told her aunt's biographer that Uncle Ted had rarely made a decision without talking it over with Aunty Bye, whose house on N Street was not too far from the White House. It was a woman's role of which she approved.

When later she joined the newly founded Junior League, she came to be regarded as its hardest worker. She was not an "angel in the house" type as New York society preferred its young women to be, but she managed to envelop work and acceptance of responsibility in the garments of a soft-spoken, soft-eyed grace and good manners so that no reputation of bluestocking or crusader attached to her.

Her other model in adolescence was Mlle Souvestre, daughter of a French philosophe and headmistress of Allenswood, a finishing school on the outskirts of London for the daughters of eminent European families. Sou, as Eleanor called her, was a woman of flashing wit and wide learning whose milieu was the upper echelon of cultivated western European society. Her standards of morality, propriety, and learning were irreproachable. Even a ruptured love relationship with the co-mistress of the school at Fontainebleau that had preceded Allenswood was spoken of by the eminent in French society as the great "tragedy" in Souvestre's life. Of this aspect of Souvestre's personality Eleanor never spoke a word, and we are left to speculate whether she ever knew about Sou's lesbianism.

The landscapes of childhood and youth are peopled, as one becomes older, with figures of mythic proportions, but often there are documents that bring us closer to realities. Soon after Eleanor, 15, arrived at Allenswood, Souvestre wrote Mrs. Hall that the girl showed a rare "purity of her heart." She commented on "the nobleness of her thought" and added, "I have not found her easily influenced in any thing that was not straightforward and honest." There was, too, a "sympathy for all those who live with her." They were perceptive words, and Eleanor's progress at Allenswood in the affections of both classmates and staff is another contemporary record that enables later generations to judge the impact she made at the time. The reciprocal devotion between Eleanor and Mrs. Cowles, and between Eleanor and Mlle Souvestre, is a measure of Eleanor's intentions in 1900 when both she and the century were young. Although society then prescribed a subordinate public role for women, she appreciated these two just because they were in history's main-stream.

It was the beginning of a century in which the United States, under the leadership of Eleanor's uncle, was becoming an actor on the world scene. As a student in England whose upper class had contributed the largest quota of girls to Allenswood, she was made quite aware of the Boer War, but from a special perspective: Sou's sympathies were with the Boers, and while the English girls cele-brated Britain's final victory Eleanor was among the handful who gathered around Sou to lament the Boer defeat. There were smaller events, at least so they appeared at the time, that transformed most individual lives even more dramatically—the spread of the use of the electric bulb, the telephone, and, soon afterward, the horseless carriage. Eleanor was conscious of these transformations. Toward the end of her life, at one of the picnics she organized for, among others, her grandchildren, she reminisced about her childhood. She told how her grandfather, the first Theodore Roosevelt, a hand-some, bearded man who reminds us of his granddaughter, built a house on Fifty-seventh Street just off Fifth Avenue, and how in 1873 Freddy Weekes, who lived on Washington Square and whom she knew as the family's lawyer, was invited to the housewarming. That was an overnight trip; his mother cautioned him and was disbeliev-ing when he said that he would be back the same night. She remem-bered Mrs. Weekes as a gentle, charming lady who "once danced with Lafayette." When she recalled such episodes, the transforma-tions of the twentieth century materialized in Mrs. Roosevelt's per-son.

Eleanor returned in 1902 to the United States after three years with Mlle Souvestre. As New York society sought to engage her in its rituals, she presents us, according to her own accounts of her coming-out, with an image of outer serenity and inner terror. Only occasionally did she reveal the anguished inner self. She did so to her "Auntie Corinne," Mrs. Douglas Robinson—her father's younger sister, an accomplished poet, and the mother of "little" Corinne, whose first months at Allenswood overlapped Eleanor's last. "Eleanor came to see me," Mrs. Robinson wrote her daughter at Allenswood. "[Her] path is not all roses. She burst into tears and said 'Auntie, I have no real home,' in such a pathetic way that my heart simply ached for her."

About this time young Franklin Roosevelt, handsome and debonair, an upperclassman at Harvard, the apple of his mother's eye, entered Eleanor's life in earnest. He seemed to Eleanor an

LEFT: *An early summer at Campobello. The woman with her is her Aunt Maude.*
RIGHT: *Eleanor and Franklin in 1906 on the porch of a cottage that belonged to Franklin's mother, Sara.*

This photograph was in the possession of Laura Delano, one of Sara's younger sisters.

improbable suitor, although her cousins on her father's side regarded this sixth cousin once removed, whom in their diaries they called "hypocrite" and "feather duster," as getting the better of the bargain. In any case, Franklin's determined courtship and Eleanor's hunger for a home and family and desire to experience everything that was the lot of women routed all doubts. When Grandma Hall asked whether she really loved Franklin, she solemnly answered yes, though in her autobiography, which appeared in 1937, she qualified that affirmative, writing, "it was years later before I understood what being in love was or what loving really meant."

Did she mean to distinguish, as she sometimes later did in talking to friends, between the "infatuation" stage of a relationship and the intimacy that grew out of the shared vicissitudes of family life? Or did she mean to imply a lack of erotic feeling? She had been brought up to regard the marriage bed as a duty and burden and may well have meant that at that time the element of sensuality was lacking on her side. All her relationships were characterized by care, solicitude, and helpfulness. She destroyed his courtship letters, perhaps because she found too painful the contrast between his youthful avowals of "fear nothing and be faithful unto death" contained in a poem he sent her that she quoted and his stratagems of escape from intimacy of later years. But we do know that in accepting him she quoted Elizabeth Barrett Browning's line "For life, for death" and felt it meant the same to him as it did to her.

Franklin's mother, Sara Delano Roosevelt, or Cousin Sallie, as Eleanor called her, handsome and convention-ruled, now entered the life of this love-hungry girl. She had a fortune of her own and was still in widow's mourning when Franklin's courtship of Eleanor began. She had lived happily, as far as we know, for almost a quarter of a century at the side of a husband twice her age and at his death focused all her devotion and possessiveness on her only child. She did not want him to marry. Even more, she did not want him to marry Eleanor, "that dear child." Eleanor had her own methods of winning by yielding, and Franklin had a will of his own. And while he did not quarrel with Mama (the accent was on the second syllable), he had learned early to keep his own counsel and to win by avoidance, or the tactics of proper timing.

They were married on St. Patrick's Day at the house of Cousin Susie (Mrs. Henry Parish, one of Eleanor's Ludlow relatives) on Seventy-sixth Street, east of Fifth Avenue. TR in place of his dead brother Elliott gave the bride away. His vibrant personality dominated the ceremony as it did the country, for he was the first occu-

Eleanor with Sara, about 1904. "... I do so want you to learn to love me a little," Eleanor wrote to her.

In her wedding dress. She and Franklin were married March 17, 1905, in the house of Eleanor's Cousin Susie (Mrs. Henry Parish). Her Uncle Ted gave her away.

The honeymoon trip to the Swiss and Italian Alps began in June. The two snapshots of Eleanor were taken by Franklin.

In Hyde Park shortly after the trip. He had to finish the year at Columbia Law School.

pant of the White House to make the presidency a daily presence in the nation's homes. Franklin, though young and a great admirer of Cousin Ted, did not like to play second fiddle to anyone, especially at his own wedding. He had the flair, the looks, the temperament, and the wiles to keep everyone else in the shadow as time went on, including the girl he married that day.

Eleanor, spirited and strong-willed, concentrated on making her marriage a success. When she and Franklin told Sara of their intention to get married, she was aware of what a shock they gave her and afterward wrote: ". . . I do so want you to learn to love me a little. . . . You must know I will always try to do what you wish. . . ." Friends remember those first years of her marriage as the period when Eleanor in dutiful attendance to her mother-in-law was wont to reply to the older woman, "Yes, Mama" or "No, Mama." Her submission to her mother-in-law paralleled her meekness to Franklin at that time. In the Dolomites, on her wedding trip, she writes in her autobiography that she was "jealous beyond words" when a charming Miss Kitty Gandy joined Franklin on a mountain-climbing jaunt that she had declined.

Jealousy—was it the fruit of her insecurity and a sense of incapacity as a woman? The conviction had been drummed into her by her mother's derision of her as "Granny," a word Franklin had picked up. (Had she told him about it during one of the exchanges of deep secrets that accompany courtship? Or was it Mama, who had known her parents, who had remembered the name?) There came a time when Eleanor accepted without too much agony other women giving him pleasure, but that was a hard discipline to master, as difficult as her belief that he must love only her. And even then she had learned to keep such instinctual responses deep down.

Beneath the subordination and surrender to her husband and mother-in-law, however, were an awareness of her own abilities and a fierce pride in her own family that led her to resent appraisals by her husband's or, more particularly, her mother-in-law's household. The conflict between the sense of her own competence and her feelings of ineptitude came out strikingly when they moved into a house on East Sixty-fifth Street that adjoined Mama's and had been built by her and given to them as a Christmas present. Three years earlier, in 1905, returning from Europe, they had moved into a house near Mama's that she had found and rented for them. By 1908 Anna and James had been born. In preparation for the latter confinement, Eleanor wrote out instructions for Franklin that were a model of a well-organized mind, and it ought not to have surprised Frank-

On the steps at Hyde Park. She was the knitter. Their first child, Anna, was born in May 1906.

lin that when they moved into the new house she should burst out sobbing, saying that this was not her house, she did not plan it, and it was not the way she wanted to live. "You were never quite sure when she would appear, day or night," she said of Sara's materializations through the doors that connected the drawing and dining rooms of the two houses. Neither Franklin nor Sara had consulted her during the house's constuction, and she had not wanted to live surrounded by servants as the scale of the house required. Above all, she had begun to resent her mother-in-law's proximity. She was a good organizer. She liked to be a doer. That conflicted with Mama's desire to have Franklin's family dependent upon her. "I think she always regretted that my husband had money of his own from his father and that I had a small income of my own," Eleanor said later. Their son James said of his grandmother's use of money, "For years she squeezed all of us—Father included—in this golden loop."

The submission to Mama that her composure masked had consequences in a tightening of lines around her mouth and her "Griselda moods," when she withdrew into heavy silence, a passive form of reproach that she did not dare voice. It is possible to put too much blame on Sara and the social code that she represented for many of the things Eleanor did in the early years of marriage and later regretted. She, too, carried a large measure of responsibility. In some respects New York society had no more obedient practitioner of its codes. Sara was only partly to blame for the parade of governesses who insulated Eleanor from her children, and when she herself took charge the result sometimes was a nursery equivalent of the Groton water cure, such as when she tied Anna's hands at night to keep her from masturbating or placed her daughter in a wire cage outside the window so she would have fresh air. Other young wives considered her daring, but the experiment was aborted when some neighbors protested.

Her joys and painful experiences as a young upper-class wife were no greater than those of her bridesmaids, all of whom were marrying at the time, and she had a strong sense of security in Franklin and her family. Having finished Columbia Law School, Franklin was marking time as a beginning lawyer, often at the Harvard and Knickerbocker Clubs. He owned one of the first Fords around, open windshield and cranked by hand, and was still admiring of Cousin Ted—whom he and Eleanor had again visited just before he turned the White House over to Taft—yet mindful that his father had been a Cleveland Democrat. He went on frequent sailing and hunting expeditions, often accompanied by Eleanor's brother Hall, who had

Eleanor and Franklin are fourth and fifth from the right in the bridal party at the marriage of Helen Roosevelt, daughter of Franklin's half-brother, "Rosy," to Theodore Douglas Robinson, son of Eleanor's Auntie Corinne. In the Rose Garden at Hyde Park, June 18, 1904.

TOP: *The Roosevelts with friends at Campobello, 1906.* BOTTOM: *Anna, a one-year-old between happy parents. The Scotty's name was Duffy.*

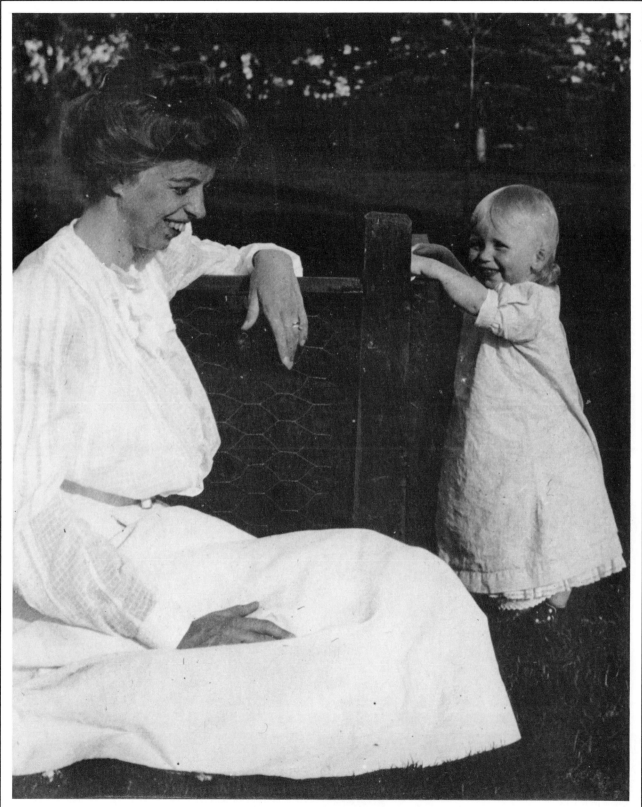

"My lady Anna is the mischief itself," wrote Eleanor. The photo was taken by FDR.

had a brilliant record at Groton and Harvard. Long summers were spent at Campobello, a Canadian island off the northeasternmost part of Maine, living at first with Sara and then in 1908 buying the house next to hers, Eleanor's first home of her own. Franklin's letters to her when he was not there were affectionate and concerned with "Babs," Franklin's nickname for her, and the "chicks." Both he and Eleanor had voices and styles that reflected good manners and patrician upbringing. Her voice had a lilt that sometimes shrilled; his was hearty and resonant. People thought of them as an attractive pair. A few of their closest friends lamented Eleanor's submissiveness to Sara but concluded that was a price she was willing to pay for marriage to Franklin and again having a family of her own. On the eve of his entry into politics, she wrote, "Dearest Honey, . . . I miss you dreadfully. . . . having other people wouldn't do any good for I just want you!" Many years later she told an interviewer: "Success in marriage depends on being able when you get over being in love, to really love. . . . You never know anyone until you marry them."

In 1910 Dutchess County Democrats were looking around for a candidate to run for the state Senate, in that heavily Republican district. They asked Franklin D. Roosevelt, young, personable, and wealthy, to do it. He, ambitious, aggressive, and gregarious, was eager to take on the fight. It would be uphill compared with the race for the Assembly he had hoped to make. Patterning himself on Theodore Roosevelt, he began the climb toward the presidency.

Of this drastic shift from an assured if unexciting career in law to the hazards of politics, Eleanor, 26, the mother of three children, of whom one had died, wrote: "I listened to all his plans with a great deal of interest. It never occurred to me that I had any part. I felt I must acquiesce in whatever he might decide and be willing to go to Albany."

Politics was man's business, and in this particular case he embodied the push and élan associated with the male animal, and she was the model of wifely subordination. She considered men superior beings and was opposed to women's suffrage, which by 1910 had considerable support in the country. Vassar College, only a few miles from Hyde Park, was a hotbed of suffrage sentiment. Yet Eleanor's admission that she listened to his plans suggests a greater passivity than may have existed. When State Senator Roosevelt brought to their house in Albany the group of insurgents he helped organize to challenge Tammany Boss Murphy's right to hand-pick who would be chosen by the legislature to succeed United States

The family grows. James is on his mother's lap and Anna on her father's. Eleanor sent copies of this photograph to the Allenswood schoolmates with whom she stayed in touch.

TOP: *Anna, Sara, and Eleanor on the* Half Moon *at Campobello in 1909.* BOTTOM: *Eleanor with Franklin Jr. and John at Campobello in 1925.*

Senator Chauncey M. Depew, she was ready. She was the gracious hostess who night after night served beer and snacks to the group of men of many backgrounds who otherwise might have been beyond her ken. She resumed the education in democratic values that had been interrupted when she abandoned her work on the Lower East Side to marry Franklin and start a family. Theodore Roosevelt wrote Franklin: "Just a line to say we are all really proud of the way you handled yourself. Good luck to you! Give my love to dear Eleanor." For the latter, the fight with Boss Murphy had been a lesson in the complexities and seamier side of politics.

In 1912, when Franklin fell ill while running for reelection, she took on briefly the management of the final weeks of the campaign before she too became sick. She worked with Louis Howe, the diminutive newspaperman who had allied himself with Franklin's fortunes. Neither she nor Mama wholly approved of Louis, but she did what had to be done. Politics in a democracy is a great equalizer. It was one of the mechanisms by which America worked as a "melting pot," in this case on Eleanor and Franklin, scions of Knickerbocker society at one end and of Al Smith at the other.

In mid-1912 she accompanied Franklin to the Baltimore convention of the Democratic Party, where the party's conservatives leagued behind Champ Clark were in deadly combat with the party's more progressive elements behind Woodrow Wilson. As the convention deadlocked, she wrote, "If we are not going to find our remedies in Progressivism then I feel sure the next step will be Socialism." It was a statement prescient of the position that she and Franklin came to symbolize as the democratic alternative in the century's grim conflict between communism and fascism. Behind the protestations of innocence and naïveté was an appraising heart and mind of which Franklin was the beneficiary. She was content to remain in the background, a position he preferred. She found the convention, moreover, tedious, its oratory meaningless, and left the sessions to take her children to Campobello. Her dislike for the convention spectacle always remained with her. As one of her friends of later years said after she was known throughout the world, success in private affairs always seemed more important to her than success in public matters.

Albany's special advantage for Eleanor was the respite it gave her from Sara's solicitude. For the first time in their married life she was not around, although she visited them often. Eleanor relished the independence Mama's absence gave her and met the obligations of a wife of a public official with her usual mixture of private terrors and public dispatch.

LEFT: *Circa 1920 from Anna R. Halstead's collection.* ABOVE: *Eleanor (without hat) at a picnic, Campobello, August 1913. She enjoyed picnics and loved to organize them.* BELOW: *A younger Eleanor, in Switzerland at the turn of the century.*

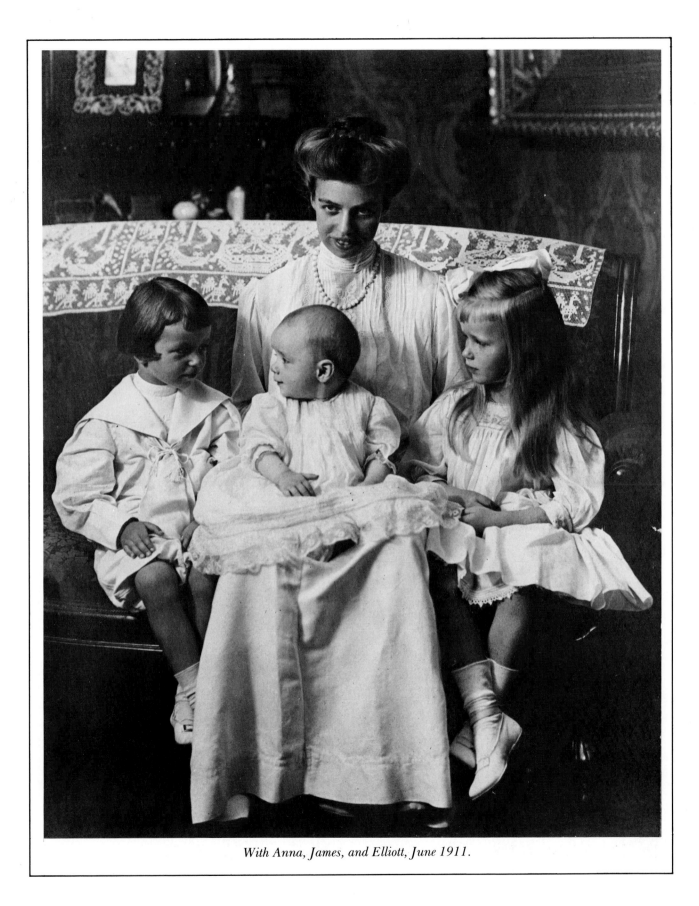

With Anna, James, and Elliott, June 1911.

ABOVE: *The sailor suits on the two boys were a favorite when their father was assistant secretary of the navy.* RIGHT: *Four generations: Grandma Hall, Mrs. Stanley Mortimer (Aunt Tissie), Eleanor (standing), and Anna, who is looking at a copy of Theodore Roosevelts's magazine* The Outlook, *August 1913.*

It was just as well that illness sidelined them both during the closing weeks of the 1912 presidential campaign, in view of their strong personal feelings for Eleanor's Uncle Ted. He had been unwilling to accept the verdict of the Republican convention and ran against his successor Howard Taft and Woodrow Wilson on a Progressive or Bull Moose ticket. He came in ahead of Taft but lost to Wilson, and though Franklin supported the latter the meaning of TR's campaign was not lost upon either Franklin or Eleanor. His campaign demonstrated that reform or liberal or progressive politics had a mainstream constituency. Sara, whose voluminous diaries said almost nothing about politics, registered the events that meant the most to her family. "Governor Wilson has a landslide. Franklin is elected with about 1,500 majority."

Franklin's eyes were set on Washington, and together with Eleanor and Sara he went to Wilson's inauguration. There he ran into Josephus Daniels, homespun editor, pacifist, prohibitionist, and newly appointed secretary of the navy. Daniels asked the "attractive young man" whether he would like to become his assistant secretary, and Roosevelt accepted with enthusiasm, for it was another position that Theodore Roosevelt had held prior to that of president. He is "our kind of liberal," Daniels told the president. He was confirmed on March 17, 1913, a day of happy memory, he wrote Eleanor, for it was the anniversary of their marriage and he only regretted that "you could not have been here with me."

By the time they left Albany, he was the public man while the family revolved around her. She quietly superintended their many moves between Albany, Hyde Park, New York, and Campobello— "an army on the march," a friend called the three children, their governnesses and servants, the trunks, valises, and hatboxes. She did it with a minimum of fuss and already had the reputation in the family of crowding an unbelievable number of jobs into her daily schedule. Despite her self-deprecation, her appearance was attractive. She was tall, with a slimness accentuated by the high choke collars and broad hats she wore. She was wasp-waisted and had masses of wavy honey-brown hair that together with sympathetic blue eyes— which even she said she was glad her children had inherited—offset a receding chin and a less pronounced version of the overly prominent teeth of Uncle Ted. An unblemished complexion, long, tapering fingers that she used vividly, and the lilt and vigor of her voice and walk all added to a quiet radiance.

Her books emphasize the decisions Franklin took in which she played no part. That disclaimer, too, has to be taken with a grain of salt. For as Franklin wrote to Eleanor's Aunt Maude, the youngest of her mother's sisters and closest to her age, urging her to come to Campobello and keep Eleanor company, ". . . I am afraid I am sometimes a little selfish and have had her too much with me in past years and made life a trifle dull for her really brilliant mind and spirit."

2

A SENSE OF
IMPENDING
CHANGE

The young Roosevelts arrived in Washington in 1913 and quickly became the beneficiaries of Theodore Roosevelt's ideas and friends as well as his New Nationalism, and at the same time adherents of Woodrow Wilson and his New Freedom. They also rented Aunty Bye's house on N Street. Eleanor continued to play an essentially private role, but as the wife of the assistant secretary of the navy there were official obligations and rituals, all of which she performed punctiliously, for they combined duty and helpfulness. "I've paid 60 calls in Washington this week and been to a luncheon at the Marine barracks," she wrote Maude soon after her arrival. ". . . I've received one long afternoon next to Mrs. Daniels until my feet ached. . . . We've been out to dinner every night, last night a big Navy League affair. . . ." Perhaps the most interesting note her letters sounded when she accompanied Franklin to Raleigh, North Carolina, was in a letter to Maude: "There seems to be so much to see and know and to learn to understand in this big country of ours, and so few of us ever try to even realize that we ought to try when we've lived in the environment that you and I grew up in."

Under the impact of Franklin's political necessities and the promptings of her heart and curiosity, she was beginning to outgrow the limitations and taboos of a society that sought to preserve its rule by its exclusiveness. She had a long way to go. Blacks were a breed apart, not to be used even as servants. As late as the mid-thirties, echoing her Georgia forebears, in her innocence she referred to blacks as "darkies," a word she meant affectionately but that gave offense. Jews were exotic and made her uncomfortable, and, in lesser measure, Catholics caused her to be on guard. It was all part of her white, Anglo-Saxon, Protestant upbringing. Even among WASPs there were distinctions of wealth and lineage. Franklin had asked Louis Howe to join him in Washington as his confidential assistant at the navy. Louis had come happily, bringing his family, but Eleanor kept them at arm's length and did not make them intimates of her household until the twenties. She made the well-descended Lucy Mercer, lovely-looking but poor, her social secretary, and though Lucy was a Catholic, sometimes had her to dinner when she needed an extra woman.

They were welcomed by Washington's top society—the old capital families and the ranking government officials, most of whom were also social register and in the diplomatic milieus. Invited to nearly all the big parties, Eleanor found herself making conversation with Justice Holmes—"brilliant and full of theories and epigrams"—and Vice President Marshall—"a good deal of a socialist with a desire for the millenium and it seems to me no very well worked out ideas so far of how we are to get there."

Whatever she might say publicly, to confidantes like Maude her judgments were terse and acute. She was a moralist, and to Franklin and Maude expressed herself pithily. As her comment on the Vice President Marshall's "socialism" indicated, she already thought of politics as the art of the possible, where goals had to be related to the means of achieving them. But she was not forward in voicing her views even within their own circle of friends. The closest of such friends met informally on Sunday evenings when Eleanor dispensed scrambled eggs done in a chafing dish, cold cuts, dessert, and cocoa.

William Phillips recorded the impression that Eleanor and Franklin made on him and his wife, Caroline. He was a protégé of Colonel House and assistant secretary of state under William Jennings Bryan. His wife, the granddaughter of Mrs. Astor, was an old friend of Eleanor's. "I knew him then," Phillips later wrote of Franklin, "as a brilliant, lovable, and somewhat happy-go-lucky friend, . . . I doubt if it ever occurred to any of us that he had the makings of a great President. . . . [and of] His wife, Eleanor, whom we all admired, [as] a quiet member of the little group. She seemed to be a little remote, or it may have been that Franklin claimed the attention, leaving her somewhat in the background." But an outstanding member of the "Club," as they called themselves—namely, Wilson's Western-bred interior secretary, Franklin K. Lane—wrote Eleanor just before he died in 1921, "I will not belittle my own feelings by saying that I have a wife who thinks you the best Eastern product—

and probably she'd move to strike out the word Eastern." She was quiet, but when she spoke the perceptive in Washington listened.

In 1914 Franklin Jr. was born at Campobello and in 1916 John in Washington. That was the end of her pregnancies. Her son Elliott claims that thereafter she ceased to share the marriage bed because neither she nor Franklin knew any other method of birth control. Innocent as Eleanor was, that is difficult to believe, and there is no other testimony to that effect.

Eleanor blamed herself for the way she brought up her children. She sought to play with them, to be their guide, to teach them to concentrate, as she had learned at Mlle Souvestre's, to speak French, to be self-reliant, and to accept pain stoically, but she thought later she had "enforced a discipline which in many ways was unwise." "She felt a tremendous sense of duty to us," Anna later said, ". . . but she did not understand or satisfy the need of a child for primary closeness to a parent." Her children's "wildness" scared her, for it revived memories of her self-indulgent father and uncles. "Let the chicks run wild at Hyde Park," Franklin counseled her, and, at Campobello, "Oh, let them scrap. It's good exercise for them."

Eleanor's real antagonist in bringing up her children was her mother-in-law, to whom "we chicks" appealed, wrote James, when "Pa and Mummy" denied them something. As Eleanor wrote bluntly in an article *McCall's* published posthumously, Sara was "determined to bend the marriage to the way she wanted it to be. What she wanted was to hang onto Franklin and his children; she wanted them to grow up as she wanted. As it turned out, Franklin's children were more my mother-in-law's children than they were mine." This judgment was all the harsher in that it was written twenty years after Sara's death, at the end of Eleanor's life.

Eleanor did not spare herself. She was partly to blame for knuckling under to Sara as long as she did. Others saw the older woman's competitiveness and viewed Eleanor's deference more sympathetically. "Caroline was always impressed," wrote William Phillips, "by Eleanor's willingness to efface herself so that there would be no trouble between mother and son. It was her thoughtfulness of other people rather than of herself which made it possible to preserve a calm and tranquil attitude in such domestic difficulties."

By the time her last son was born she ceased being tyrannized by nurses and governesses and with her last two children achieved a playfulness and intimacy she had denied herself in earlier years. At the same time, the urgencies of a world war thrust private considerations into the background. In the twenties, when she began to

speak out for hers   on
her experiences in   uch
candor and purpo   specially among wome   ther
she spoke out as a   ker,
she had something

    With the outb   and
nationalist, was in   velt
of Admiral Alfred   wer
to national influer   , an
apostle of prepared   f the
Allies, particularly   the
western front, an a   ting
with a group oppo   n of
Josephus, called "be

    Eleanor's views matched those of her husband, but there were important qualifications. Soon after the war's outbreak, Carola von Passavant, a classmate at Souvestre's and a German aristocrat, asked her how she felt about Germany "in this war." Eleanor replied that

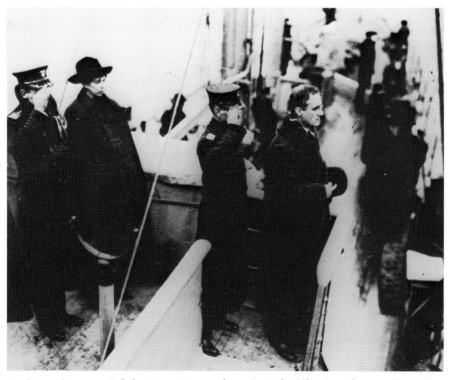

Assistant Secretary of the Navy Roosevelt reviews the Victory Fleet *on its return from Europe, December 26, 1918. A gaunt Eleanor is second from the left.*

she hated war but was not a pacifist, a position she maintained all her life. "This whole war seems to me too terrible," she wrote Carola. ". . . every people believes that it is right. . . . I wish it [war] could be wiped from the face of the earth though I recognize that in our present state of civilization there comes a time when every people must fight or lose its self-respect. I feel that it is almost too much to expect that we shall be spared when there is so much sorrow and suffering in so many countries abroad."

In 1915 William Jennings Bryan resigned as Wilson's secretary of state to lead a countryside peace campaign. Franklin exulted in Bryan's departure from the cabinet. Eleanor was glad that Bryan was out but admired "his sticking to his principles," an attitude that she found rare in politics. Looking back at the period in her autobiography, she wrote, "Anti-war germs must have been in me even then." But she was vigorously pro-Ally, impatient with Wilson's careful reactions to Germany's U-boat campaign, and comfortable with Franklin's leadership of the preparedness faction in the administration.

They moved in pro-Ally circles, one of their best friends being "Springy," Sir Cecil Spring Rice, poet and British ambassador. He had been best man at TR's wedding and knew both of Eleanor's parents. She and Springy got on particularly well and her demurral (if any) to his cynicism about Wilson's motives were mild. Yet Wilson's plea at the beginning of his second term for a "peace without victory" and a postwar order based on self-determination, disarmament, and freedom of the seas elated her. "I think the Allies are wild but it may be successful," she wrote Sara in a departure from Franklin's and Uncle Ted's interventionism.

Hopes for a negotiated peace were finished when Germany launched unrestricted submarine warfare and relieved the Allies of the necessity of rejecting Wilson's bid. Soon afterward, Wilson went to Congress to declare war. "I went," wrote Eleanor, "and listened breathlessly and returned home still half-dazed by the sense of impending change."

3

GOING PUBLIC

"THEN WE WENT into the war," she told Lorena Hickok, a reporter for the Associated Press who had been assigned to cover her during the 1932 presidential campaign. "Instead of making calls, I found myself spending three days a week in a canteen down at the railroad yards, one afternoon a week distributing free work for the Navy League, two days a week visiting the naval hospital, and contributing whatever time I had left to the Navy Red Cross and the Navy Relief Society." Mama's sister dubbed her the "willing work horse," and the Food Administration suggested to the Times that it interview her as a model of conservation in large households. The reporter made light of her well-heeled thrift, as did Franklin: ". . . I am proud to be the husband of the Originator, Discoverer and Inventor of the New Household Economy for Millionaires. . . . all Washington is talking of the Roosevelt plan." Eleanor protested the reporter's coverage: "I never will be caught again that's sure and I'd like to crawl away for shame." American history has treated the episode generously as an illustration of Eleanor's innocence rather than of the "conspicuous consumption" of the upper classes; it was a measure, however, of the distance she still had to travel in her acceptance of an America as a commonwealth of equal rights and duties for all.

Her cousin Alice, as contentious and self-absorbed as Eleanor was self-effacing and considerate, said of this period in Eleanor's life that she "went public." Eleanor and Alice were contrasts in character. Talented personalities both, their polarities reflected differences in the American psyche, the individualist and the solidarist.

Alice's spite notwithstanding, Eleanor's wartime work showed a developing readiness to initiate and administer as well as a willingness to do the donkeywork. It was Alice whose sharp eyes detected Franklin's romance with Eleanor's secretary and promoted it. She relished taking her virtuous cousin down a peg. "He was married to Eleanor," she said of his *affaire de coeur*. "He deserved it." Eleanor was destined for leadership whether the Lucy Mercer affair happened or not. But it did, and the doubts and self-disgust its discovery caused, the insecurities it revived, the loneliness it bred, seared her permanently.

She rarely spoke about the Mercer affair, but the references to its impact on her are unmistakable. "There was a war then too," she wrote the author during World War II, " & the bottom dropped out of my own particular world & I faced myself, my surroundings, my world, honestly for the first time." Her insecurity stayed with her, covert but real.

Eleanor offered Franklin his "freedom," as Alice and other family members stated it. Anna, in an unpublished account at the Roosevelt Library, says that she heard from her mother that "she asked that he take time to think things over carefully before he gave her a definite answer. . . . He voluntarily promised to end any 'romantic relationship' with Lucy and seemed to realize how much pain he had given her." Her motives in holding her marriage together were many, but the children were paramount, as they were with him. In accepting a compromise arrangement, she felt she had ruled out the possibilities of real happiness. So it would seem judging from her advice to a friend for whose mood of "lonely despair" she felt deep sympathy: "I beg you not to accept ½ loaf of love." It was fortunate for the United States and the world that the two stayed together, but she paid a price in forever searching for the "oneness" that she considered the basis for a happy married life.

In the diary she kept during their first stay in Washington, one line screams out from the page: "Went to Church but could not go to communion." She and Franklin stayed together, but his choice of a younger, more beautiful woman over her became an ache that never left her. Yet as she later wrote, "the hardest blows of fate, met with courage, somehow are bearable." She felt that people who faced such ordeals honestly emerged stronger and more caring. The poem "Psyche" by Virginia Moore, which she clipped from the newspaper and on which she wrote "1918" and always kept with her, charted the course of her own feelings that year.

The soul that has believed
And is deceived
Thinks nothing for a while,
All thoughts are vile.

And then . . .

Finding the pull of breath
Better than death . . .
The soul that had believed
And was deceived
Ends by believing more
Than ever before.

"Somewhere along the line of development," Eleanor later wrote, "we discover what we really are & then we make our real decision for which we are responsible. Make that decision primarily for yourself because you can never really live anyone else's life not even your child's. The influence you exert is through your own life and what you become yourself." The traits that were always there—above all, helpfulness, which is a form of love—now had a wider focus.

A period of intensive education in new realities began for Eleanor Roosevelt. It coincided with America's posing major challenges to American women—what they would do with the vote they had gained in the passage of the suffrage amendment and how they would view America's role in the world, the abolition of war especially. She would be a major participant in shaping the answers to both.

She and Franklin were reconciled. They remained a family. The bringing up of the children and management of the household continued to be her job. Where she could be of help to him, she would. Affection both had in abundance, but they renounced certain marriage claims on each other, and that for her loving nature was the hardest of all disciplines to master. A woman of strength and grace, she had been humbled. The taboos and blinders of social exclusiveness fell from her eyes. One does not give oneself airs, she later said. She was resolved to work, with him where possible, alone when necessary. She would learn to cook, to type, to take shorthand. She made a renewed attempt to drive a motor car. She refused any longer to be shielded from the world's business.

The war ended, and she accompanied Franklin on his second tour of Europe's naval installations, this time on demobilization arrangements. The trip brought them to the Paris Peace Conference, which for the moment was the focus of the world's hopes that it had indeed been a war to end war. Eleanor "swept Mrs. [Woodrow] Wilson up in her project of visiting the war wounded in the hospitals," Mrs. Wilson's social secretary wrote. She and Franklin toured the eerily quiet, ravaged battle areas, where she felt the ghosts of the men who had fought there always beside them. Her hatred of war as a method of settling disputes became a ruling passion. They returned on the same boat as Wilson, partisans of the newly drafted Covenant of the League of Nations that he was bringing back with him. "What hopes we had that the League would really prove the instrument for the prevention of future wars," Eleanor said of their reaction to the Covenant. "Little did we dream at the time what the future held."

When on their return to the United States Franklin went off to

Sara, Franklin, and Eleanor, 1920, at the end of his term as assistant secretary of the navy.

Elliott sits just below his father. Franklin Jr. and John are in the front with Chief, Anna's dog. Sitting on Eleanor's left is James, and in front of them is Anna. Sara is at center.

Nova Scotia with her brother Hall on a hunting expedition, she was glad to attend the Industrial Conference, convened amid a rash of postwar strikes to find a *modus vivendi* between labor and industry. It failed, but here were real problems and she enjoyed being involved. She invited the American delegates to an International Congress of Working Women, a "radical gathering," to lunch with her. The pattern of making personal friends of the people who staffed the movements she wanted to work with had begun.

It was a trying period for her personally. "Mama and I have had a bad time," her diary read. "I should be ashamed of myself and am not." She reported a "stormy evening" with Mrs. Parish. Both women upheld society's exclusiveness and rigidities. There were strained silences with Franklin. But they stayed together and as the Wilson years drew to a close prepared to return to New York together.

Franklin went to San Francisco to the Democratic convention in the summer of 1920 and she and the children to Campobello. There she heard that he had been nominated for vice president as running mate of Governor Cox of Ohio. She came to Hyde Park with Anna to hear Franklin offically accept the nomination. "Essentially a home woman," the *Times* wrote; but when a Poughkeepsie reporter a few weeks later asked her about her political views, her answer conveyed a different picture: "Yes, I am interested in politics. . . . My politics? Oh yes, I am a Democrat, but"—here she paused—"I was brought up a staunch Republican,—and turned Democrat. I believe that the best interests of the country are in the hands of the Democratic Party for they are the most progressive." She had begun to speak in her own voice, diffidently but unmistakably for herself. Governor Cox and Franklin called on the semiparalyzed Wilson in Washington. "It is very strange not to have you with me in all these doings," he wrote her afterward. And her letters were addressed to "Dearest, dear Honey." They were lovers and strangers and would continue in that uneasy relationship until his death.

Nineteen-twenty was the first presidential election in which women voted, and Franklin asked her to join him on the campaign train, the *Westboro,* an experience that taught her much about the nuts and bolts of the democratic process. It also marked the beginning of genuine friendship with Louis Howe. At the end of a day's campaigning, Franklin and several of his aides settled down to poker as a way of easing the strains of nonstop speech making and obligatory camaraderie. Louis sensed Eleanor's loneliness and her interest in being more than an onlooker. He began to discuss Franklin's speeches and campaign strategies with her. By the end of the trip, the two of them—chain-smoking Louis, who looked like a gargoyle and planned like a Machiavelli, and the tall, queenly woman who would not permit herself airs—had become political confederates as well as friends.

The notification ceremony at Hyde Park, August 9, 1920, after FDR had been nominated for vice president. At Eleanor's right are Secretary of the Navy Joseph Daniels, the McAdoos, Homer Cummings, and Governor and Mrs. Alfred E. Smith.

Campaign trip. On far left is Louis Howe and with him is Thomas Lynch, a Poughkeepsie neighbor and campaign aid.

4

A SERVICE
OF LOVE

WHEN THEY RETURNED to New York following Franklin's defeat, Warren Harding's "normalcy" had become the word of the hour. The women's movement after passage of the suffrage amendment was in retreat, and so was the cause of peace. The Senate had rejected United States entry into the new League of Nations, and Carrie Chapman's call for a women's peace vote in the 1920 elections had gone unheeded. A period of social advance had come to an end, and the Wilsonians left Washington. The Republicans and their business ethic took over.

Eleanor and Franklin lived again in their East Sixty-fifth Street house. He went to work as vice president of the Fidelity and Deposit Company, a large surety bonding firm. "I am delighted to get back into the real world again," he told Felix Frankfurter. And she to pursue a new career of independence and self-realization. She became active in a network of organizations, many of them run by veterans of the suffrage struggles, dedicated, knowledgeable women who often lived with other women in relations of intimacy described by the nineteenth-century term "Boston Marriage."

The organizations included the League of Women Voters, successor to the National Women's Suffrage Association, the Women's Trade Union League, housing and consumers movements, and the Women's Division of the New York State Democratic party. She made personal friends in each of them—the scholarly publicist Esther Lape and the lawyer Elizabeth Read, who shared a Greenwich Village apartment and helped Eleanor in the League of Women Voters; the red-headed, tiny, militant socialist Rose Schneiderman, who directed the Women's Trade Union League; Marion Dickerman and Nancy Cook in the Democratic party, another Village twosome. The first was tall, solemn, and an educator, the other shorter, kinky-haired, spirited, an able designer and craftsman. Soon Eleanor was spending an evening a week with Esther and Elizabeth reading aloud. Rose became her teacher in the problems of trade unionism, addressing in particular the issue of women's role in industry and unions. She helped Dorothy (Mrs. Willard) Straight raise money for a League clubhouse and one night a week she taught women workers how to read. Nancy and Marion became intimate friends as well as associates in the building up of the Women's Division of the state Democratic party. She was learning one of the greatest secrets of leadership in a democracy—the involvement of others in the growth of the movements that her presence and spirit inspired.

She eagerly developed these new friends who were so different from those with whom she had grown up and entered activities with modesty. Her readiness to work and good sense enchanted all. As in the canteen work in 1917, in the Junior League in 1902, at Allenswood in 1898, she was quickly recognized as a leader. Circumstances now intervened to give her work with the Democratic women special relevance.

Franklin arrived at Campobello on the yacht *Sabalo* at the beginning of August 1921. A few days later he was stricken by infantile paralysis. For two weeks she slept on a cot in his room, ministering to him night and day, spelled only by Louis, who also was in Campobello. "She is one of my heroines," commented the specialist whom they located at Portland, Maine, but who made an incorrect diagnosis and prescribed painful massages that she and Louis gave FDR until another specialist correctly saw his disease as polio. The story has often been told how she and Louis helped him put up his tremendous fight against despair, and after the recovery of his spirits, although not of his legs, abetted him in his determination to return to politics.

The latter resulted in a dramatic showdown with Sara, who wanted her son to retire to Hyde Park and jealously fought Eleanor, using as weapons the resentment of the five children and seeking to dismiss Louis as "that ugly, dirty little man," giving Eleanor what she called "the most trying winter" in her life. "I am sorrier for you than Franklin," wrote Caroline Phillips, who was abroad but immediately understood the situation. Eleanor's self-control broke only occasionally. She remained in command and Sara's domination was ended. Franklin's illness, she wrote, "made me stand on my own two feet."

41

Had she yielded to Sara, she would have become, she feared, "a completely colorless echo of my husband and mother-in-law and torn between them. I might have stayed a weak character forever if I had not found that out."

Polio sidelined Franklin, and Louis, who had become a part of the Sixty-fifth Street household, came to her and urged her to serve as Franklin's surrogate in Democratic politics. Such a move, he said, would bolster Franklin's interest in the party and the party's interest in him. It was an argument aimed at her sympathetic nature, and it worked. At the 1922 state Democratic convention she led the Dutchess County delegation—which included Henry Morgenthau, Jr., who with his wife Elinor had become friends as well as neighbors—three times around the hall behind Smith-for-governor banners. By the time of the following state convention, her repeated tours of the upstate areas to nurture clubs of Democratic women resulted in a large turnout for a women's dinner in Albany, where she led those attending in a successful revolt against male monopolization of power.

"It is always disagreeable to take stands," she rallied the women in her high-pitched, deeply earnest tones. "It is always easier to compromise, always easier to let things go. To many women, and I am one of them, it is extremely difficult to care about anything enough to cause disagreement or unpleasant feelings, but I have come to the conclusion that this must be done for a time until we can prove our strength and demand respect for our wishes." The men capitulated. "It was Mrs. Roosevelt," the *New York Times* noted in an editorial, "a highly intelligent and capable politician," who introduced the Smith resolution at the convention. She was less successful a few months later at the national convention when her subcommittee of women, although until early morning stationed outside the doors of the Resolutions Committee, was unable to get inside or to arrange a hearing for its child-labor resolution.

Another focus of self-education in the twenties was the help she gave Esther and Elizabeth in conducting a nationwide competition for the best practicable peace plan, for which Edward M. Bok, the publicist, offered a "princely" prize to the winner. A total of 22,165 entries were received. It provoked a Senate inquiry led by isolationists into what they denounced as an "internationalist" plot. The three women read every entry, an education in itself. Even Franklin drafted a plan, which he did not submit because of his wife's membership on the directing committee but which reemerged in later years in his thinking about a charter for the United Nations. Eleanor's antiwar speeches at the time emphasized gradulism in international affairs and United States entry into the World Court as a step toward membership in the League of Nations. Avoid "panaceas," she urged a convention of women's clubs, and "grasp anything which is a step forward. . . . all big changes in human history have been arrived at slowly and through many compromises." That was the basic spirit with which she approached efforts to regulate relations among people and nations. It kept her in the mainstream of politics. How much she learned from Franklin and how much he learned from her can only be surmised.

Steadily she developed as a speaker, coached constantly by Louis. He edited her drafts, gave her pointers in delivery, and sat in the back of the hall preparing his critiques. Her knees quaked, but only she, and perhaps Louis, knew, and gradually she was recognized as a woman with interesting views that she presented spiritedly and always as "the willing worker." She was active in Hyde Park and Dutchess County affairs. Such neighborly activities were worth doing on their own, and if they had merit had much wider influence, she felt. She was equally active in the affairs of New York City, chiefly as a member of the Women's City Club. In 1924 Mary W. "Molly" Dewson became its civic secretary. Molly had supervised parole for girls in Massachusetts, gone to France as a Red Cross worker in the war, helped Felix Frankfurter prepare the economic briefs in several minimum-wage cases, and with her companion Polly Porter lived in the same cooperative house in Greenwich Village as Nan Cook and Marion Dickerman. A commanding figure, she immediately impressed Eleanor. During the period 1924–28 Eleanor was active in the Club's monitoring of the state legislature in Albany and on its regional planning and transit committees, and in the election debates the Club held for its members, she spoke for the Democratic candidates—for Robert F. Wagner as senator in 1926 and Alfred E. Smith for president in 1928. She resigned from the Club's board after Franklin was elected governor but agreed to speak on "Women in Politics" as part of a City Club series of broadcasts over the fledgling NBC network. Radio interested her as a way of reaching people, and she resolved to master its use regardless of the difficulties inherent in the learning experience.

All this was interwoven with a solicitude for Franklin's unremitting efforts to recover the use of his paralyzed limbs. She was assisted by Louis and Marguerite LeHand ("Missy"), who, after serving as his secretary in the 1920 campaign organization, had become his companion as well as secretary. He carried on a voluminous correspondence with Democratic leaders throughout the country on

Eleanor and Emily Newell Blair at the headquarters of the Democratic Platform Advisory Committee in 1924. The male-dominated Resolutions Committee rejected their proposal that it approve ratification of the Child Labor Amendment.

the direction the party should be taking. These messages were given life by Eleanor's surrogate role. "I'm only being *active* until you can be again," she assured him; "it isn't such a great desire on my part to serve the world again and I'll fall back into habits of sloth quite easily! Hurry up for as you know my ever present sense of the uselessness of all things will overwhelm me sooner or later!"

Two major decisions to build houses away from Sara's big house in Hyde Park overlooking the Hudson—hers at Val-Kill and Franklin's in Georgia—shaped each of their lives. Franklin became interested in some curative springs in Georgia and after careful consideration bought them and the rundown hotel attached to them. Under his personal supervision, a major rehabilitation center for polio victims was developed. Warm Springs became his second home. Eleanor had misgivings. She did not want to discourage him, and she knew that efforts to slow him down had to be stated in terms acceptable to his self-esteem. Her sympathetic, gentle phrases came naturally. "I know you love creative work, my only feeling is that Georgia is somewhat distant for you to keep in touch with what is really a big undertaking. One cannot, it seems to me, have *vital* interests in widely divided places but that may be because I'm old and rather overwhelmed by what there is to do in one place and it wearies me to think of even undertaking to make new ties. Don't be discouraged by me; I have great confidence in your extraordinary interest and enthusiasm. It is just that I couldn't do it."

There were other reasons why she stayed away from Warm Springs. Although her Bulloch ancestors hailed from the vicinity, she did not like the white-supremacy attitudes that still prevailed there. Moreover, it was Missy's bailiwick; she had accompanied Franklin on the Florida houseboat sojourns that preceded his discovery of Warm Springs. Eleanor was grateful to her because it enabled her to be with the children and to lead her own life. She treated Missy as one of her children and repressed her feelings of jealousy. She was learning to permit others to do for Franklin what she was unable to do herself. "How can she permit him to do that?" friends would ask themselves when he and Missy went off together. But as long as neither was able to give the other the warmth and sense of sharing each needed, she steeled herself to pay the price in loneliness. She appeared at Warm Springs only rarely.

Franklin understood his wife's loneliness and his inability to give her the companionship she wanted. He also understood and sympathized with her need to protect herself against his mother. So he encouraged her "and some of her political friends," as he put it, to

Franklin with Eleanor and Sara: Inauguration Day as governor of New York, January 1, 1929.

use some of his land over the Val-Kill creek, two miles east of Mama's big house, "to build a shack" and to dig out Val-Kill "so as to form an old fashioned swimming hole." The friends with whom she went into this enterprise were Nancy and Marion, and by New Year's Day 1926 they were having their first meal, sitting on nail kegs in the newly built fieldstone cottage. Val-Kill and Warm Springs represented the way Eleanor and Franklin were drifting apart. A shared interest in their five children, his need of her in politics, and her need of his buoyancy and optimism to keep from yielding to a sense of the hopelessness of things that she had had to fight ever since her orphaned childhood kept them together.

So it was in September 1928 when at the Rochester state convention she put in a call for Al Smith to Franklin at Warm Springs that enabled the governor to persuade her husband to head the New York ticket in a year that looked bleak for the Democrats. She adamantly told everyone that she made no effort to influence Franklin's reply. "My husband always makes his own decisions." Yet in her account of what happened, she wrote, "I sometimes wonder whether I really wanted Franklin to run." Did she mean that the time had arrived for Franklin to play a more active role? It was the impression of Edward J. Flynn, the Bronx Democratic leader who was Smith's liaison with the Roosevelts, "that she would be happy" if he consented to run. Or did she mean that her own withdrawal from political activity that Franklin's return to politics portended was not altogether to her liking?

The outcome of the 1928 race was an overwhelming defeat for Smith as president and a paper-thin victory for Roosevelt in New York State. Eleanor was so deeply involved in the Smith campaign, heading up the work with the women, that to a reporter who asked her the day after election how she felt about her husband's victory, she replied, "If the rest of the ticket didn't get in, what does it matter? . . . No, I am not excited about my husband's election. I don't care. What difference can it make to me?"

Restrained by a sense of the uselessness of things, she was at the same time propelled forward by the desire to be effective. Though at the time it did not seem to her she had accomplished much, FDR's victory owed a great deal to her. But her husband would never acknowledge that and she would never claim it, so the sweet taste of success was withheld.

5

ELEANOR'S SECRET

From the time Mlle Souvestre spotted Eleanor's "purity" of heart and "nobleness" of thought, her qualities of self-effacement had been noted. In the twenties her affections had moved onto a wider stage. Her statement to the reporter about her husband's surprise election seemed out of character. However indifferent to success for herself she professed to be, she always wanted it for others if that was what they wanted.

So what did her remark mean? She gave some explanation to Elinor Morgenthau. "I felt Gov. Smith's election meant something but whether Franklin spends 2 years in Albany or not matters as you know comparatively little. It will have pleasant and unpleasant sides for him & the good to the State is problematical. Crowds, newspapers, etc. mean so little, it does not even stir me but I know it does others."

She had developed her own views with such a flair for apt statement that magazines asked her for paid pieces. One such article in 1927 had been written for *Success* magazine. Her willingness to write for a journal with that title suggested, as did the subject itself, "What I Most Want Out of Life," that she was not indifferent to achievement.

The article stressed the usefulness of political activity as a safeguard against the emptiness of women's lives, especially after their children were grown. "Home comes first. But—in second and third and last place there is room for countless other concerns. . . . And so if anyone were to ask me what I want out of life I would say—the opportunity for doing something useful, for in no other way, I am convinced, can true happiness be attained."

There was another hint that being useful, especially in politics, gave her pleasure and that Franklin's election to the governorship was not an unmixed blessing for her personally. Perhaps her seeming indifference to Franklin's election hid something else—her distress at having to give up or modify her own work. "I resign now, with regret," from the Women's Division of the Democratic State Committee," she informed Elinor Morgenthau, "only because I know if I take any part in politics everyone will attribute anything I say or do to Franklin & that wouldn't be fair to him." The same reluctance to abandon the interests and activities she had developed since her return from Washington was evident in the arrangements she made to move into the executive mansion in Albany.

Circumstances shape us, she often said. But her example illustrated an unstated part of the proposition in which she believed equally: how men and women adapt to life's changes is even more important than evaluating their achievements. The return to Albany with Franklin and her response to it was such a change. She strengthened Franklin in his determination to be his own man, not Al Smith's, in the governor's chair. She resigned from all activities that seemed competitive with Franklin in politics and sought ways to help him that he considered acceptable and did not raise the charge that "she wore the pants," a charge as upsetting to Franklin, especially as it was not true, as it was to her and the public. She also superintended the movements of her five children, remembering not to be "executive," as she called that tendency in herself. Anna was married, James at Harvard, a rebellious Elliott and the two youngest boys, Franklin Jr. and John, were at Groton.

The "grandest room" in the executive mansion she gave to Franklin, and the bedroom she assigned to Missy was larger than her own, "as if," wrote Marion Dickerman later, "to emphasize that she considered her 'first lady' duties to be less important than others she performed in her own right as Eleanor Roosevelt." Marion and Nan were her closest friends at the time, and her decision to spend half her week in Albany and half in Hyde Park and New York was rooted in her friendship with them. She loved the stone cottage at Val-Kill that the three had built and the furniture factory that they had started there, in part to give employment to local people and of which the talented Nancy was the sparkplug and she the indefatigable saleswoman. Hesitantly and then with joy she taught three days

TOP: *Eleanor supervises work in the furniture factory at Val-Kill. The shop was part of the Val-Kill Industries that she, Nancy Cook, and Marion Dickerman organized in the twenties. When it was closed during Eleanor's years in the White House, she converted the workshop building into a cottage for herself.* BOTTOM: *Teaching gave her a great deal of pleasure. She retained her ties with the Todhunter School in New York City. Here, the 1933 graduating class visits the White House. Second from left, Nancy Cook; fifth from left, the principal of the school, Marion Dickerman; far left, Eleanor's secretary and the woman who "made life possible for me," Malvina Thompson.*

a week at Todhunter, a private school in Manhattan where Marion was the principal and she the vice-principal. Nancy Cook continued to direct the Women's Division of the state Democratic organization, so Eleanor's resignation was nominal, and though she took her name off the masthead of the Division's "News," she continued to edit it. Elizabeth Marbury, whom the newspapers always telephoned when they wanted "a woman's view," had said, "They won't need people like me. They've got their Mrs. Roosevelt now." Eleanor had never consciously pushed herself forward, was ready at all times to withdraw, and impressed a *New York Times* interviewer as "the strongest argument that could be presented against those who hold that by entering politics a woman is bound to lose her womanliness and charm."

The self-fulfillment she had begun to experience and was scarcely able to acknowledge even to herself still seemed to be tentative, and episodes such as one that occurred in 1930 involving Mama and Franklin Jr. at Hyde Park could be shattering events. She had planned to take young Franklin and John to Europe driving in her own Chevvy, Nan and Marion in their Buick. Mama objected. The sons of the governor should be seen in a nicer vehicle. During the discussion, Franklin Jr. commented teasingly about his mother's having once driven them into a tree. She fled the room in tears, and Franklin sent their son out to apologize. She later wrote Franklin Jr., after he returned to Groton, how difficult it was for her who as a child had been afraid of everything to overcome such fears as driving, swimming, or camping, "or to feel I could hold any opinion, even against a nurse. I suddenly have gone back & I imagine I'm too old now to pull back."

She was made of tougher stuff, and though she ordered a chauffeur-driven Daimler to be ready to meet them when they docked in England, she did not give up driving or any of the other skills she had mastered. Just before she and the boys departed from Montreal, she accompanied Franklin on "the good ship *Inspector* which has a glass roof" along the Barge Canal. On that trip, under his tutelage, she took his place going through the state institutions at which they stopped, learning the arts of inspection, which meant getting around the cosmetic appearances that officials put up for her. She mastered the skill of making trenchant reports to Franklin. It was part of her becoming a sort of ombudsman in his administration, an unelected office into which her energy and heart impelled her and which was added to by her insistence on answering all letters that came addressed to her and to speaking wherever she was asked.

She wanted to be involved, but she also valued her newly won independence. That ran into Franklin's insistence on being himself. So though they were civilized and well-mannered, the process of sharing did not go easily. The male attitude, she had once said, consisted of loving and honoring the woman: "I'll give you all the freedom you wish and all the money I can but—leave me my business and politics." Franklin must have been in her mind when she said that, and she had armored herself against his rebuffs. That is why the friendship with Nan and Marion prospered. When his self-preoccupation verged on indifference to her, she took refuge with the two in the stone cottage at Val-Kill. Once her "Griselda" mood lasted three days until Nan and Marion had talked, teased, and cajoled her out of it. Then they telephoned Franklin at the big house, and he drove over in his specially built Ford. She went out and talked with him, and then, said Marion, they drove off together. Years later Eleanor said to a young friend that all women have a desire to be first in someone's life and that men's failure to recognize that accounted for many of the strange things that women sometimes seemed to do.

Nan and Marion helped keep the marriage going because they felt that at bottom that was what Eleanor wanted. Together with them she did many things she would have hesitated to do alone— the Val-Kill industries, Todhunter, the Women's Division. Without her participation the activities would have passed unnoticed, if, indeed, they were done at all. It is equally true that without Nan and Marion and her desire to help them in what they wanted to do, she might not have involved herself.

Although she had resigned from all committees, she was more rather than less in demand as a speaker around the state. Thus it happened naturally that Roosevelt assigned one of the state troopers, Earl Miller, to accompany her. He had guarded Al Smith and now him. He was handsome, a marksman, boxer, and rider. "He gave something to Eleanor," Marion said, and soon the two were the warmest of companions. "You know it was a very deep attachment. . . . It was very, very deep. . . . He used to annoy me the way he talked to her. I didn't like his tone of voice when he told her what to do, or when he did not like what was being served at the table. . . . When Earl first came to the Big House with the Troopers he would eat out with the servants. That changed and he was later eating with the family."

Earl became dear to her because he too helped her conquer her job as the first lady of the state. He too helped her overcome her timidity, and she began horseback riding, swimming, driving a car, using a revolver. Even his "manhandling" had its appeal. Two of Eleanor's sons believe there was a romantic attachment between Eleanor and Earl and Marion said Eleanor flirted with the idea of marrying him. Perhaps so. He of course denied it. She encouraged his romances with younger women and he portrayed an affair he had with Missy as an effort to break up her relationship with the governor as a favor to "The Lady." Somewhere in her psyche she was not as indifferent to Missy's relationship with Franklin as she had appeared to be.

Caroline Phillips described Eleanor and Franklin during the governorship years after she and her husband visited them in Albany. She had known Eleanor since the turn of the century, and her diary gives a flavor of the "extended family" the two built around themselves and that seemed to fuse naturally into the larger concepts that Franklin sounded when he began his bid for the presidency—the concept of interdependence and of the country as a "seamless web." When Earl Miller came to tea, Caroline wrote, she called him "Major" and thought he might be an aide. There was "a secretary" whom all called Missy and who was "a very nice young woman." The atmosphere in the mansion was relaxed and hospitable, a friendliness that was particularly borne in on the Phillipses after dinner when a movie was shown and the governor and Eleanor and their guests were joined by the household servants. They drove down to Hyde Park, where they were met by "Eleanor's great friend, short, stocky Miss Cooke [*sic*] with her poppy-out blue eyes and short wiry grey hair . . . [who] was as always warmly embraced by Eleanor.

"She [Nancy] is a most determined person . . . who now runs the Val-Kill furniture factory at Hyde Park, as well as the Roosevelt family!" Their two friends were "living on *top* of their arduous job in a magnificent way. . . . The only flaw I could find in Eleanor is her disdain for any interest in food. . . . She was laughing at her mother-in-law who wanted to discuss with her what dishes would be most delicious for a dinner party, 'as though,' said Eleanor, 'anyone nowadays had time to spend twenty minutes planning what to eat.'"

Roosevelt's reelection victory exceeded all forecasts. It was a victory in which, according to the plain-spoken Molly Dewson, "Mrs. Roosevelt was a very great factor." For Eleanor, Franklin's sweeping victory in upstate rural New York brought "a greater satisfaction" than anything else. Her goodnight note to her husband after the sweep that made him frontrunner in the Democratic bid for the presidency reflected the abiding affection between the two. "Much

Louis Howe told her in 1934 that if she wanted to be elected president after FDR finished a second term she should tell Howe so that he could begin to plan. She laughed off the proposal. The country was not ready for a woman as president, she said, and she was not interested in elective office for herself.

love & a world of congratulations. It is a triumph in so many ways, dear & so well earned. Bless you & good luck these next two years."

But she learned of Franklin's decision to try for the nomination in 1932 from Louis and not her husband. Although she loyally supported the Friends of Roosevelt organization, which was directed by Louis and whose associate director became Molly Dewson, she did not achieve the warmth and intimacy with Franklin for which she hungered. Franklin had to go abroad to see his mother, who was ailing in Paris. "We are really very dependent on each other," she wrote him, "though we do see so little of each other." The closer Roosevelt moved toward nomination, the more compromises he felt he had to make on issues such as prohibition, the League of Nations, child labor, even the pace of unemployment relief. Some of Roosevelt's advisors considered Eleanor "dangerously unrealistic," and he had his own ways of distancing himself from her.

Her unhappiness brimmed over. Louis went out to Chicago, where, together with James Farley, he directed the Roosevelt operations at the nominating convention. Nancy Cook was also there. "I know she didn't want him to run," Marion said later. "She wrote a letter to Nan in Chicago saying that she could not live in the White House. Nan showed it to Louis and he tore it into a thousand pieces. . . . There were times when life became too much for her."

"I'm the agitator; he's the politician," Eleanor later would say. The men he assembled about him, including the members of the Brain Trust, were annoyed by her frequent efforts to direct conversation at the dinner table, usually to advance some "good cause," as Rexford G. Tugwell, the most leftward leaning of the group, wrote. Sam Rosenman, Franklin's counsel and speech writer, and Doc O'Connor, his law partner and political advisor, considered her a menace, Doc once astonishing Tugwell with the observation to the Brain Trust group that it was their job "to get the pants off Eleanor and onto Frank." Even Tugwell, although he acknowledged that her views "went cautiously in the right direction," found them lacking in profundity. She did not deliberately set out to become America's conscience as Franklin, his advisors, and the Democratic party approached national power, but that was what her sense of duty and strength of character mandated. She was loyal to Franklin, rendered him "a service of love," and that service required that she speak up honestly. As the nation plunged toward economic paralysis, she insisted on presenting her own views. She did so with poise and composure. But as she confided to a new friend, Lorena Hickok, the AP reporter who had been assigned to cover her, on her forty-eighth birthday in 1932: "I'm a middle-aged woman. It's good to be middle-aged. Things don't matter so much. You don't take it so hard when things happen to you that you don't like."

The outside world would not have guessed she dreaded going into the White House. Grace Tully, Missy's assistant, reported the scene in the governor's study when the call came through from Chicago that California had switched and assured Roosevelt's nomination: "Mrs. Roosevelt and Missy LeHand embraced each other. Both embraced me. John and Elliott tossed scratch paper in the air and shook hands as if they hadn't seen each other in years. Mrs. Roosevelt came down out of the clouds before the rest of us. 'I'm going to make some bacon and eggs,' she announced."

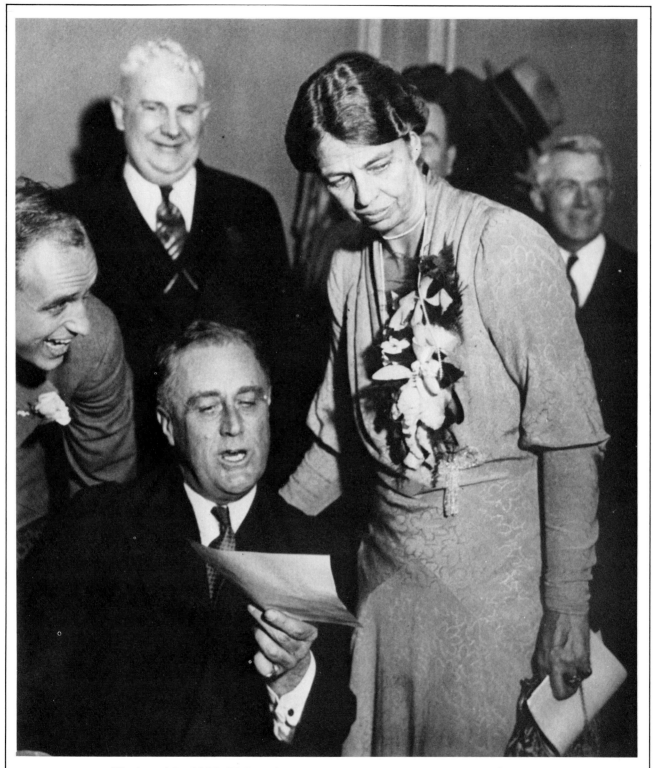

Election night, 1932. FDR reads victory telegram to Eleanor and James, on his left.

6

AN INDEPENDENT
FIRST LADY

I NEVER WANTED to be a President's wife, and don't want it now," she told Hickok after Franklin's election. She was aware her statement would be read throughout the country, and she wanted it to be. "For him, of course, I'm glad—sincerely. I am a Democrat, too. Being a Democrat, I believe this change is for the better." Behind this disavowal of ambition to be first lady was another set of sensations, her sense of being an outsider. This feeling of separation was confirmed when just before his inauguration he turned aside her offer to serve as a "listening post" for him and handle part of his mail. That was Missy's job, he rebuffed her, and in her account of life with Franklin in *This I Remember*, written after his death, she commented, "I knew he was right and that it would not work, but it was a last effort to keep in close touch and to feel that I had a real job to do."

The life force, denied one channel by circumstance, altered its course. There would be no "First Lady of the Land," she said to Hickok, only "plain, ordinary Mrs. Roosevelt. . . . Now I shall have to work out my own salvation." Resigned to the criticism that she considered inevitable, her attitude about being herself was "I can't help it," and she proceeded to transform the first lady's role into a unique force for good.

Her breaks with precedent had been foreshadowed during the time between Roosevelt's election and his inauguration on March 4. When she had come down to Washington to look over the White House, she declined to be accompanied by a military aide or be driven there in a government limousine. Instead she walked from the hotel.

LEFT: *She was unhappy at the prospect of becoming first lady, she confided to close friends, but in public she put on a brave front. Here she is seeing Franklin Jr. off to Europe in July 1932.* RIGHT: *The first lady-elect in December 1932. It was before unemployment relief, the WPA, and other New Deal measures had transformed the face of depression America, and soup kitchens were an accepted part of the landscape.*

At the White House she briskly informed the chief usher of what she and Franklin wanted during the first days of their occupancy and "rattled it off as if she had known it her whole life," the admiring man said. In New York City the Women's Trade Union League gave her a farewell dinner. It was thronged with the civic leaders with whom she had worked throughout the twenties. "Perhaps I have acquired more education than some of you [who] have educated me realize," she told the audience, and in a few simple words outlined her intentions: "I truly believe that I understand what faces the great masses of people in the country today. I have no illusions that anyone can change the world in a short time. Things cannot be completely changed in five minutes. Yet I do believe that even a few people, who want to understand, to help and to do the right thing for the great numbers of people instead of the few can help."

Heywood Broun, whose column was "must" reading for liberals, defended her right to be herself. He was "delighted to know that

December 25, 1932, on the eve of their entry into the White House.

*FDR greets his wife on her return from a trip, March 17, 1934, their wedding
anniversary. Eight years later, returning from war-torn Europe, she would write:
"We looked out . . . and knew that FDR had taken time off to come and meet us. . . .
I really think Franklin was glad to see me back."*

Eleanor and Franklin on the Hyde Park lawn. Despite the internal tensions, they were a team.

we are going to have a woman in the White House who feels like Ibsen's Nora, [that] she is before all else a human being and that she has a right to her own individual career regardless of the prominence of her husband."

A month before Roosevelt's election, a month as black as any as the depression approached its nadir, she had done a magazine article on the meaning of religion, writing: "The worst thing that has come to us from the depression is fear. Fear of an uncertain future, fear of not being able to meet our problems, fear of not being equipped to cope with life as we live it today." She had her antidote, and rooted in it was the basis of her democratic faith: "The fundamental vital thing which must be alive in each human consciousness is the religious teaching that we cannot live for ourselves alone and that as long as we are here on this earth we are all of us brothers, regardless of race, creed or color."

On a gray, chilly inauguration morning, she joined Mrs. Hoover in the limousine to drive down Pennsylvania Avenue to the Capitol behind the president and president-elect. Across the Atlantic,

Hitler had just come to power in Germany. In the United States, economic paralysis had set in. She heard her husband's resonant voice proclaim: "This Nation asks for action and action now. Our greatest primary task is to put people to work." To meet the unprecedented emergency, he was ready, he said, to ask Congress to give him wartime powers if necessary. Here the applause was greatest.

It had been "a little terrifying," she told Hickok, who awaited her return at the White House. "The crowds were so tremendous, and you felt that they would do *anything*—if only someone would tell them *what* to do." One had a "feeling of going it blindly" in the onrush of events and "the important thing . . . [was] to accept and share with others whatever may come. . . ."

That first evening there was a family party, and she was at the front door to greet the seventy-five guests, including Alice Longworth. Her cousin, an amusing mimic, was entertaining Washington with a takeoff of Eleanor as a speaker. But Eleanor's poise and good will disarmed all malevolence. She invited Alice to do her parody for her and thanked her for the helpful demonstration.

Her own sensible, unforced approach to the behavior expected of a first lady was even more evident in her decision to hold regular press conferences. Hickok suggested she do so, and she was encouraged by Franklin and Louis. She restricted it to women in order to further employment and to underscore that she was not attempting to encroach on Franklin's domain. She appeared at the first with a large box of candies, which she passed around—a symbolic gesture that in later days might have been misunderstood but that against the austere, reclusive background of the Hoovers was appreciated for the friendliness it represented.

She soon made personal friends of the regulars at such sessions, though not at the expense of their objectivity. A well-meaning reporter who cautioned her that an answer might get her into trouble was criticized by her colleagues, and Mrs. Roosevelt herself disagreed with such admonitions. "Sometimes I say things," she told her press conference, "which I thoroughly understand are likely to cause unfavorable comment in some quarters, and perhaps you newspaper women think I should keep them off the record. What you don't understand is that perhaps I am making these statements on purpose to arouse controversy and thereby perhaps get the topics talked about and so get people to thinking about them."

The reporters appreciated being treated as human beings. Many who came to Washington often "lost the human touch if they ever had it," a reporter wrote her in gratitude. She was a friend as well as a news source and was dubbed "God's gift to newspaper women" after she organized a Gridiron Widows' buffet for newswomen, since the Gridiron Club's annual dinner, which the president attended, excluded them.

Her warmth and readiness to do the sensible, if unconventional, thing became legendary. Once when she took Louis for their regular afternoon drive, he directed her to the encampment to which the veterans of the war had returned seeking payment of a bonus after being driven from Washington the year before by President Hoover and General MacArthur. She left Louis in the car and proceeded to tour the rows of tents, stood on the mess line, and after an impromptu speech in which she reminisced about her own wartime experiences ended up singing with them "There's A Long, Long Trail." "Hoover sent the army. Roosevelt sent his wife," remarked a left-wing veteran who was watching the influence of the Communists dwindle before his eyes. She was her husband's surrogate, but the way she carried out such missions was her own, and the country began to appreciate that and watch for it.

In the depths of the depression, she advocated nourishing but inexpensive menus and had the White House set an example in their use. She campaigned against sweatshops. She urged women to shop where decent working conditions were provided. She called for the elimination of child labor and advocated more money for teachers' salaries. On the eve of the World Economic Conference, with foreign dignitaries trooping in and out of the White House, she addressed her press conference with an anti-isolationist plea whose intensity impressed the hard-bitten press corps. "We've got to find the basis for a more stabilized world. . . . We are in an ideal position to lead, if we will lead, because we have suffered less. Only a few years are left to work in. Everywhere over there is the dread of this war that may come."

Her entry upon the Washington scene was made easier by the presence of her friends. She had settled Louis in the capacious Lincoln bedroom across the hall from her own sitting room. Malvina Thompson, "Tommy," a plain-spoken, highly competent woman who had become her regular secretary during the governorship years, was more than a secretary. She was counselor, haven for the children, companion on trips about the country—the woman, she later said, who made life possible for her. Nan was in and out helping her furnish the White House and get settled.

Marion, busy with Todhunter, nevertheless received the elegantly penned invitations to diverse White House affairs. So did Esther

TOP: *With Earl Miller at his camp in the Adirondacks in the autumn of 1934.* BOTTOM: *Riding with her youngest son, John. She bought her horse, Dot, from Earl Miller; it was stabled at Fort Meyers.*

and Elizabeth. The former's foundation was at work on "Relations of Record" between the United States and the USSR. "Hurry up," Franklin had urged her, fueling Esther's hopes that America was about to end its nonrecognition of the Bolshevik regime. Eleanor's Dutchess neighbor Elinor Morgenthau came to Washington with her husband, who, by the end of the year, was named secretary of the treasury. She and Elinor, a friend whom she cherished, rode almost daily in Rock Creek Park.

Earl had remained behind in New York, a chief inspector of the state's prison and parole guards. He had married in 1932, in a "well-publicized" ceremony, as he put it, in order to end the gossip about him and "The Lady." Eleanor and Franklin were in attendance, Anna was bridesmaid, and Elliott best man. He had not loved the girl, and the marriage was foundering. He still was high in Eleanor's affections and already Eleanor and Earl were planning two weeks "off the record" in the mountains in northern New York with only Nan and Marion along.

They were all friends who had helped her education, who sustained her in the difficult role she had elected to play as an independent first lady who served Franklin, walking the corridors of power and remaining a human being. An important addition to the group had been Lorena Hickok, Eleanor's confidante during the campaign. The letters exchanged between the two, in their frequency as well as in their ardent expressions of endearment, revealed an attraction of startling intensity. It more likely was erotic on Hickok's part, especially since she had other lesbian relationships, but the point seems almost irrelevant in view of Franklin's indifference to Eleanor and the unquestioned feelings of tender passion with which Eleanor invested her solicitude for Hickok. Whatever the dynamics of her adjustment to the first lady's role that she had wanted desperately to avoid, unburdening herself to Hickok helped her out emotionally. Her gratitude was reflected in the almost daily letters, all in longhand, that she sent to Hickok and that taken together comprise a diary of the New Deal.

Another change in Eleanor's life was the growing elegance of her clothes. In the twenties it had seemed often that she cared no more about what she wore than about what she ate—tweeds, a hair net, and a blouse were all that she needed. But now the nation's top couturiers took charge, and she spent more time—though perhaps not much more—on the selection of what she wore. In 1934 the nation's dress designers chose her as "the best dressed woman in the

United States," a title that Eleanor said was the "funniest" and "grandest" of accolades.

Another effort to improve herself resulted from acceptance of a bid by a voice teacher to give her exercises that would develop resonance and depth of tone. She worked with Mrs. Elizabeth von Hesse throughout the White House years and fulfilled her teacher's promise, "You could project your voice without losing any of its beauty."

By the end of Roosevelt's first year, the mood of the country had changed. Eleanor shared in the adulation that flowed toward the White House from a reviving people. But it was more than that. She as much as her husband had come to personify the Roosevelt era. Bess Furman had ended her story about Mrs. Roosevelt's debut as first lady with "Washington had never seen the like—a social transformation had taken place with the New Deal." And Cissy Patterson, the publisher of the *Washington Herald,* whom Eleanor had known in her debutante days, ended an interview with Eleanor on an unusual note of admiration: "Mrs. Roosevelt has solved the problem of living better than any woman I have ever known."

7

"MY
CONSCIENCE
BOTHERED
THEM"

Some suspected that her busyness was meant to fill a vacuum that might not have existed if FDR had reciprocated her love. Her days seemed to be planned so as never to allow her to be alone, and when she was alone she immersed herself in the papers piled high on the Val-Kill desk she had brought down. There were reports and manuscripts to read, articles and letters to be written, the latter in the thousands, many to friends and children. Long after everyone but the Secret Service agents had gone to sleep, she worked at her desk. It was as if she discovered her inner voice in these dialogues with the people she loved. She defined herself in relation to other people. "We are the product of the choices we have made," she often said, but meaningful choices required self-knowledge, which she described as the ability to look at oneself honestly. Until one could do that, one was unable to be sympathetic with or understanding of others.

Always available to people and to causes, she soon became one of Washington's legends. She was not just a "prism" who reflected light brilliantly although herself "rooted in nothing," as John Maynard Keynes said of Lloyd George, but a woman for whom doing good was second nature, the only addiction, a friend remarked, that did not carry a hangover. Asked by a magazine to comment on "What I Hope to Leave Behind," she quoted Robert Louis Stevenson's Christmas Sermon: "To be honest, to be kind—to earn a little and to spend a little less, to make upon the whole a family happier for his presence, to renounce when that shall be necessary and not be embittered, to keep a few friends but these without capitulation—

above all, on the same grim condition, to keep friends with himself—here is a task for all that a man has of fortitude and delicacy." The words were epigraphic of her life:to renounce—was it Franklin—without bitterness; to have friends—was she thinking of Hick?—without capitulation; above all, to keep friends with herself. Here was "consciousness raising" long before the term was used.

Four large two-room suites were at the corners of the second floor of the White House. Hers was in the southwest, Louis's in the northwest. Franklin's bedroom and Oval Study were next to hers. From her desk by a tall window that overlooked a magnolia planted by Andrew Jackson, the view swept across lawns to the Washington Monument. There she sat, a pool of quietness, in a sitting room that once had been Lincoln's bedroom and was filled with memories of him: ". . . often I have thought of how he must have walked that floor, wondering about the ultimate outcome of the people and their struggles and their sufferings in his day."

Before she went to bed, she wrote letters, "and sometimes that is very late." Then she took her dogs for a walk around the White House grounds. She drank in the beauty of the White House, its graceful proportions, stately windows, soft lights—a house, she thought, that belonged to all the people. She usually was up at 7:30 and either did exercises or rode in Rock Creek Park. Frequently there were guests at breakfast, but when she saw the breakfast tray going in to Franklin, she excused herself and went into his room to say good morning. Often she left a letter or received his reply to one she had left the night before, or asked a question, or discussed the children or the world. Breakfast over, she saw in turn the chief usher, the social secretary, and the housekeeper. Then Malvina Thompson bustled in. She had gone through the mail and selected the letters she knew her boss would want to see immediately. There were 300,000 pieces of mail that first year, and Eleanor loved it. There were telephone calls, articles, replies to be dictated. Louis, acting as her agent, made a contract for her to do pieces for the North American Newspaper Alliance and a monthly page for the *Women's Home Companion*. As in the twenties, when she had disciplined herself to teach at Todhunter, she now schooled herself to reach all groups, using every medium—newspaper columns, magazine articles, books, the radio, the stage, the press conference.

She thought of herself as a journalist, and the words PRESS RATES COLLECT, with which she started her daily copy, were among the nicest of her day, she thought. She glowed when her editor called her "a real newspaper person," proudly carried a membership card of the American Newspaper Guild, asked and received handsome fees, and, when a bout of illness felled her, declined to allow the president to do her column for her, roguishly advising her readers, "We want to pass it on to you so that you will realize what you missed, but we refused courteously and rapidly knowing that if it once became the President's column we would lose our readers and that would be very sad."

Even before Franklin was governor, she had tirelessly toured New York State; now that he was president, she did the same nationally. Soon she had a lecture agent, and while she had set speeches on several subjects infused them with her spontaneity and warmth. Each time that she arose to speak, she prayed silently that she might have something meaningful to say to the people in front of her. She focused on faces in her audiences and learned the knack of sensing and shaping their moods.

She had difficulty with the formal receptions and entertainments at the White House but made peace with such obligations by telling herself, "It is really the position which is invited and not the person!" It was not Eleanor Roosevelt, the person, whom officials were anxious to meet, but the "wife of the President." "Try it sometimes," she drily suggested to a friend after shaking hands with 3,100 members of the Daughters of the American Revolution in an hour and a half. "I was a symbol which tied the people who came by me in the long ever-recurring receiving lines to their government."

Neither protocol nor stamina but a constant thoughtfulness explained her success as a hostess. When Rose Schneiderman came to Washington on trade union business and did not let her know, she immediately wrote: "Please always come to lunch or to see me. I always feel badly when I miss any of my friends." And Elizabeth Read commented to Esther, "Eleanor likes to have her friends with her."

Although she shrank from the limelight, her whole life was on public display. She avoided direct party activity of the sort in which she had engaged before Franklin became governor, but she was intensely interested in the political scene and was a recipient of as much information in Washington as anyone except Franklin. One must never stop learning, she asserted up until she died. She eschewed power for herself but understood its uses for good purposes, especially the pivotal nature of politics in a democracy. She knew the ways of politicians and officials and eagerly embraced the role of making people feel that the government was *theirs* and the men and women who worked for Franklin that they were there to serve the people.

She relied especially on some people in Washington. Franklin and Louis came first as sources of information and action. Secretary of the Treasury Henry Morgenthau used her and she used him; he sounded her out about Franklin's moods and his stand on certain issues. She had come to know Harry Hopkins in the social welfare field in New York, and when he came to Washington to handle unemployment relief for the president had him to dinner and at family occasions. She encouraged the budding friendship between the president and his chief relief administrator, for Hopkins had vision as well as executive energy.

Some of her strongest ties were with the women in the administration. There were few problems of government, whether of people or policies, that she did not discuss with Elinor. Most cabinet wives had to protect their husbands and were too bland. She preferred the company of newspaperwomen. Roosevelt understood the importance of women politically and was aware, even if he did not acknowledge it, how Eleanor's leadership had redounded to his advantage. Louis understood it even more and had said to her after Franklin's election, ". . . if you want to be President in 1940, tell me now so I can start getting things ready." He saw possibilities for such a candidacy if the American people continued to divide "along humanitarian-conservative lines."

She ruled herself out. Moreover, she did not believe the time had arrived when a majority of the people trusted the judgment of a woman as president. She agreed with Louis that the entrance of women onto the political scene meant a change in American politics. Her book *It's Up to the Women,* which an enterprising publisher rushed into print in 1933, was a call to women to assume a progressive role if the nation was to come through the crisis of the depression successfully.

In addition to women's rights, her own priorities were youth; blacks and minorities generally; the abolition of poverty; and, above all, peace. Mary Beard described her positions as reaching "to the borderlands of political, social and cultural change." She left it to Washington officials to guess which of her memoranda, telephone calls, and visits were instigated by the president. Similarly, the newspaperwomen did not know when she said something as a trial balloon for the president or as gentle pressure on him. Almost all were

TOP: *Down into a coal mine.* BOTTOM: *Listening to FDR accept the Democratic nomination in June 1936. Anna is at her left, Sara at her right. "A man must come to a moment like this with a great sense of responsibility," she wrote of the event.*

With Mary McLeod Bethune and Aubrey Williams of the National Youth Administration at a national conference of Negro Youth, January 1937.

disarmed, however, by the feminine grace and patent good will with which she invested views and requests.

How much she believed or hoped might result from the programs and people she called to Franklin's attention is not wholly clear. She shielded herself against backlash by saying she was simply ventilating a view to start discussion—not because she necessarily believed in it. Yet the miseries of the depression acting on her urgent sense of duty moved her to explore some utopian schemes. She impetuously promoted *Prohibiting Poverty* by Prestonia Mann Martin, the grandaughter of Horace Mann. It borrowed the utopian Edward Bellamy's proposal for a Young Workers Corps. Its enrollees would produce the "seven cardinal necessities" for everyone, leaving its young "Commoners" free after eight years' national service to pursue wealth, fame, power, and leisure. She liked the plan, saying, "I wish they could lead us to a point where every one would have security, as far as the basic necessities are concerned." But it was simplistic and would have meant a great deal of regimentation, and she retreated when Mrs. Mann asked for an endorsement: she did not see it as a working blueprint but a stimulus to discussion.

A few weeks later Upton Sinclair, another Bellamyite, sought her support for his own plan, End Poverty in California (EPIC), which was then sweeping the state. When Sinclair, a long-time Socialist and writer, asked whether he and his wife might call on her, she received them but afterward declined to support his race for the governorship. Some of his ideas were practicable, others were not; in any case, she was unwilling to make any public statement. She was ahead of the president on many issues, but, in addition to his political necessities, to which she deferred, she had a strong streak of realism that kept her in the mainstream of democratic politics.

Her liberal ideas led the *World-Telegram,* which in 1933 had not yet turned conservative, to welcome a "connubial Presidency" as a safeguard against the dangers of presidential isolation. Arthur Krock, a pillar of American conservatism as well as a journalistic pundit, noted after watching the White House closely: "She had stronger convictions than he on the subjects of social welfare and progress. She was also a very determined woman. . . . " She summed up her own role in relation to Franklin: "I'm the agitator; he's the politician." Only rarely did he try to rein in her advocacy. "You go right ahead and stand for whatever you feel is right," was his usual attitude. ". . . I have to stand on my own legs. Besides, I can always say I can't do a thing with you."

Whatever Franklin's reservations about her strong stands, they did not apply to her major foray into the politics of reform in the early years of his administration—Arthurdale, a subsistence homestead development in West Virginia. This new town, created by the federal government to rescue and rehabilitate hundreds of miners and their families in the coal towns of Appalachia, illustrated her strengths and weaknesses as a reformer as well as her relations with Franklin. Lorena Hickok, who at the time was her closest friend, directed her attention to Appalachia. Hickok was there as confidential agent for Harry Hopkins. Her graphic reports on poverty went to Hopkins and to Eleanor, who sent many of them on to the president. Hickok's report on the despair and degradation of the miners in Scott's Run brought Eleanor into action. She drew the president's attention to the miners' plight. The creation of Arthurdale was, she said, "the President's idea." Louis Howe, too, became engrossed with it. Authorization to create such resettlements had been built into the National Recovery Act at Roosevelt's specific request; with Eleanor and Howe, he shared a desire to achieve a better rural-urban balance through planned communities. All three felt that technological advance and unrestrained market forces were creating the paradox of the huddled city and the abandoned farm.

Eleanor placed herself at the disposal of the homesteaders, and

73

TOP: *FDR sought to resettle workers from exhausted mines in new communities, of which Arthurdale was one. Eleanor involved herself in the lives of its homesteaders. Here she is leading a square dance.* BOTTOM: *At the National Education Association Day at the World's Fair in New York City, June 30, 1938.*

Arthurdale became her "special baby." Not only was it a job Franklin had given her to do, but she felt that what was done in a single community might show the way to a nation. Through her efforts, Arthurdale was going to have the best educational system in the country, a model public health service, producer and consumer cooperatives, and handicrafts and music reflective of Appalachia.

Despite her best efforts, the experiment in "Eden," as opposition papers derisively called it, failed. The Republicans denounced it as "socialistic" and succeeded in stopping the administration's efforts to establish a government-owned, job-creating factory in Arthurdale. There were doubts, too, within the administration. Rexford Tugwell, to whom the homesteads were transferred in 1935, was uneasy about back-to-the-land movements and industrial decentralization. People went to employment, not employment to people, he felt, nor was urban growth an evil in itself. He saw the resettlement and land reform ideas as ways of moving farmers off exhausted soil and using submarginal lands to create garden cities. Arthurdale seemed to him a flawed concept, and while he admired Eleanor and valued her support, he thought her "naive about many things—after all, she had a defective education."

Eleanor was the last to give up. For the president, resettlement was another experiment in reform and reconstruction. If it provoked too great resistance, keep it at arm's length, if necessary reshape it, and in the last analysis, move on to something else. That was his brilliance. He was pointed Zionward and used his incomparable sense of political strategy to involve government in plans that revived the nation.

Eleanor's exigent heart sounded in a prayer she heard in St. John's Church and reprinted in "My Day," her daily column:

> Our Father, who hast set a restlessness in our hearts and made us all seekers after that which we can never fully find; forbid us to be satisfied with what we make of life. Draw us from base content, and set our eyes on far-off goals. Keep us at tasks too hard for us, that we may be driven to Thee for strength.

She was usually in advance of Franklin in pushing for progressive legislation, but it was always done with the knowledge that Franklin was there to pull her up short when generosity and compassion pushed her beyond the pale of the politically possible. Arthurdale taught her anew that people and institutions change slowly. It was not only Republican opposition to the new communities as "socialistic" and the misgivings of social scientists like Tugwell about their conceptual basis; resistance also came from the resettlers themselves. When she enlisted educators like John Dewey in the formulation of a progressive curriculum for Arthurdale's children, she ran up against the deepest longings of the displaced miners—to be like other communities and to have their children's A-B-Cs taught as elsewhere. They were cool to the cooperative idea. "They wanted cows tied to their back fences," she said in the late 1930s. "They trusted nobody, not even themselves. They had an eye out all the time to see who was going to cheat them next." She was discouraged on another score. Too much White House helpfulness was not good either. Too many of the people in Arthurdale seemed to feel that a solution to all their problems was to turn to government. Government alone could do certain things; others should be left to local initiative. The unwillingness of local people to take their share of responsibility disappointed her.

The experience did not turn her into a conservative but reinforced an earlier realization that steadiness of will and timing were required to bring goals nearer, especially in democratic politics. It was a difficult lesson to learn for this woman of mercy. After one of Franklin's major reform bills had been rejected in Congress, she wrote a friend: "I did go up to Franklin's room and say sometimes I wondered whether people were worth saving, but his answer was not [as the friend had heard] 'Sleep on that, Eleanor,' but 'Give people time, my dear. It takes time to understand things. You are much too impatient and would never make a good politician.' "

In 1938 a reviewer of *My Days*, a selection from her daily column, wrote: "She sees bewildered young people as individuals, not as Youth; men and women out of work as individuals, not merely as the Unemployed; workers as individuals, not as Labor. She looks behind the welcoming crowds to the many people not lined in the streets." She saw individuals, not groups or abstractions; yet they were members of groups, and the causes she embraced along with them, although marginal to the interests of the powerful in the thirties, came to the forefront of the history of later decades—the rights of women, blacks, and others minorities, young people, and fledgling unions.

"About the most important letter I ever wrote you," Molly Dewson alerted Mrs. Roosevelt a few weeks after she and Franklin moved into the White House, enclosing a seven-page list of women whom she had urged James Farley, the chairman of the Democratic National Committee and postmaster general, to appoint to positions in government. Molly came down to Washington at Farley's request to run the Women's Division of the Democratic National Committee. She was quite effective with the men in securing the appointment of women to government jobs, and when Farley equivocated she brought the matter to Eleanor, who called Farley herself or if necessary asked the president to intervene. With Eleanor's help, Molly had urged the appointment of a first woman to the cabinet—Frances Perkins—and Mrs. Roosevelt's engagement books registered how she often lunched or dined with Perkins; Isabella Greenway, who had turned up in Congress; and Mary Rumsey, Averell Harriman's older sister. The latter had turned her brother into a Democrat and was head of the National Recovery Administration Consumers Advisory Board. They were all forceful women who had made it in a man's world, part of an informal women's network in Washington. Roosevelt had needed little urging to appoint Perkins, first to his cabinet in Albany, then as secretary of labor in Washington. He was sympathetic to women's advancement, but the unprecedented number of women in his administration reflected the presence of Eleanor at his side.

Whether Molly acted as Eleanor's surrogate or vice versa is less important than the recognition of women that Eleanor made possible. An informal political sisterhood emerged in New Deal Washington. It was symbolized by Molly's appearances at Eleanor's press conferences and by the appearances of other women who headed government agencies. Mary Harriman Rumsey came to speak about consumers needs. Frances Perkins announced the establishment of camps for unemployed women. "You may be sure that under the new Civil Works program [predecessor of the Works Progress Administration] women will not be overlooked," Mrs. Roosevelt assured the press. At a dinner honoring the appointment of Frances Perkins, Mrs. Roosevelt saluted her sense of service and selflessness: " . . . she is not staying because she will gain anything materially . . . but . . . as an opportunity for . . . service to . . . the workingmen and women and their families. This is what we mean as I see it by the 'new deal.' "

Long before a "gender gap" in the polls showed that women differed from men by as much as thirteen percentage points in the way that they responded to questions of war, peace, social security, civil rights, and the environment, Eleanor wrote in *It's Up to the Women* that it was women's "understanding heart" and "vitality" that gave hopes of social change.

She was always prodding Franklin to "remember the ladies," to use Abigail Adams's reminder to John as he was off to the Constitutional Convention. She was equally insistent that women work their passage in politics on the basis of ability and character, not because of male chivalry. Some day a woman would be elected president, but not "while we speak of a 'woman's vote.' I hope it only becomes a reality when she is elected as an individual, because of her capacity and the trust which a majority of the people have in her ability as a person."

She was asked in 1940 by *Liberty,* a widely read weekly, to answer the question "What Is the Matter with Women?" Its first title asked whether women ruled, but she toned that down. She showed a friend a draft, something "naughty," she said. Tommy had misgivings, she reported, about the first lady's calling the moral code man-made. "Of course, it is," she said crisply. The article began: "A man's world! Is it, or isn't it? Some people say that we American women really rule the United States of America—make our men do what we want—run our houses as we want—lead our lives as we want—run away for vacations when we want—work when we want!"

But however it seemed on the surface,

> in the long run, I think, way down deep inside of us, there is one thing that cannot be eradicated—we like to please the gentlemen.
>
> This is the basic reason why this is still a man's world. The men like to run the world and only very few women care whether they run it or not. What we women really care about is that our homes shall run smoothly, and our men be well cared for and happy.

She reviewed the dismal depression years, when working women were let go in order to create jobs for unemployed men. She ended her broadside against male rule with a characteristic display of graceful compliance laced with hints of change.

> It isn't that women haven't the brains or the ability or the physical strength to dominate. It is that they want the world the way it is and for the most part are content. What will happen when they really want something different, I hesitate to say, because I have a firm belief in the ability and power of women to achieve. It is a man's world now, however, and will be just as long as the women want it to be!

Four decades later feminism was a major component of the

ideologies of liberation. And even the internal revolt among feminists against identification of women's emancipation with hostility to sexual differentiation was in line with Eleanor Roosevelt's insights.

The problem of Negro discrimination confronted her from the moment she entered the White House. She still used words like "darky" and "pickaninny," but her advanced views on racial discrimination had kept her away from Warm Springs and its Jim Crow setting. On her visit to Appalachia she had visited black as well as white families in Scott's Run. "Some of the Negroes think she is God," a local editor wrote. But then the white homesteaders at Arthurdale refused to admit blacks. On this issue she knew she had to move cautiously, even with her husband. He wanted to improve the lot of the Negroes, but their second emancipation was not among his high priorities. He preferred to have Eleanor take the lead while he equivocated.

An early meeting of black leaders at the White House that she convened was meant to be a discussion of Negro participation in Arthurdale. The White House venue for a meeting with blacks was itself unprecedented, Eleanor's good will even more so. The discussion quickly became more general and ended in agreement that in the South desegregation, desirable as it was, should be subordinated to Negro participation in the New Deal's aid programs. The discussion ended at midnight, when the president was wheeled in and said a few friendly words.

He was less able to elude black demands for an anti-lynching bill. The pressure for such legislation came principally from the National Association for the Advancement of Colored People, led by Walter White, its executive director. Eleanor was White's willing confederate in pursuing the president until he agreed to see him. "I did not chose the tools with which I must work," he explained to the NAACP leader. White southerners controlled the strategic committees in Congress, and if he came out for the anti-lynching legislation they would "block every bill" he sent up. Anti-lynching was never on the president's "must" list.

Many New Dealers also managed to evade the problem. Washington was still a southern town. The president's appointments and news secretaries were southerners. Eleanor's racial views upset them. They feared "I might hurt my husband politically and socially"; and, indeed, by the mid-thirties leaflets were being distributed in parts of the South that portrayed her as a "nigger-lover." Their real target was Roosevelt."

Her dedication to the cause of racial justice did not diminish.

She pressed Harry Hopkins and Aubrey Williams, his assistant in the Works Progress Administration, to appoint Mary McLeod Bethune, a black educator, to head Negro youth work. Mrs. Bethune became a fixture in New Deal Washington. Eleanor was her ally and protector. Mary Bethune was, as a black policeman said of her, "as black as a black shoe," had a crinkled face, and was of matronly proportions. Only after Eleanor had pecked her on the cheek—the way she greeted many of her co-workers—did she feel she had overcome the last vestige of racial prejudice in herself.

She urged her husband to move faster, and she counseled the Negro community that "great changes come slowly. . . . it is better to fight hard with conciliatory methods." This advice was in a letter to Pauli Murray, a black student whom she had encountered in one of the first relief camps set up for women, who had spoken up to her in resentful and defiant tones, and whose friendship she encouraged because it was through individuals like Pauli that she sensed the fires burning in the Negro soul.

The most dramatic example of her stand for racial justice was her resignation from the Daughters of the American Revolution when it denied the use of its Constitution Hall for a Marian Anderson concert. ". . . [Y]ou are the first lady of the land in your own right," an admiring cousin, Corinne Alsop, a Republican legislator, wrote her. The blaze of public interest that attended her resignation made it possible for the Department of Interior, at Walter White's suggestion, to make the Mall from the Lincoln Memorial to the Washington Monument available for the concert. "Majestic and impressive," wrote Harold Ickes afterwards. "Only one thing marred it," White thanked her—"that you couldn't be there. But I understand thoroughly the reason you could not come." She was effective in gaining consideration for Negro demands and in doing so became instrumental in keeping the Negro vote Democratic.

From the time of the Works Progress Administration's beginnings, its projects, whether they benefited man or woman, skilled worker, leaf raker, or professional, writer, painter or musician, young or old, claimed her attention. Some she instigated, especially those related to youth and women; others—the Federal Theater Project, the Writers Project—she abetted. Wherever she went, her sympathetic visit seemed to confer the nation's accolade on the humblest of enterprises. Her visits often brought action, and whether the word went from headquarters to locality or vice versa, the unemployed felt attention was being paid.

She also encouraged the organizations of the unemployed, whose hunger marches enlisted her sympathy; the Workers Alliance; and the American Youth Congress. The radicals in their ranks, including the Communists, did not daunt her. When Vice President John Nance Garner grumbled that the troops should be called out if the jobless sought to march down Pennsylvania Avenue, she said in that case her place would be among the marchers.

The jobless young in particular seemed an indictment of Western civilization. "I have moments of real terror," she said in 1934, "when I think we may be losing this generation." She welcomed the establishment of the Civilian Conservation Corps (CCC), visited its reforestations camps, did not like to see them administered by the army, and sought a broader solution such as universal youth service. Society could not say to the million young people who left school each year that it had no use for them. "[A] civilization which does not provide young people with a way to earn a living is pretty poor," she wrote in 1934. Frances Perkins estimated the number of young people between the ages of eighteen and thirty who were out of school and out of work at 3,300,000. Eleanor pressed government leaders, especially Hopkins and Williams, to set up a national youth agency. They feared its establishment might raise the cry that the president was trying to regiment America's youth the way Hitler was doing. She brought it to the president, and he responded that if it was the right thing for young people, it should be done and he would risk the criticism. The result was the creation of the National Youth Administration (NYA). "You have got to decide what you want in this country," she told the graduating class of the University of North Carolina. "I know that all of us would like to see a country in which there is no poverty, in which every one has a minimum income on which a decent standard of living can be maintained." New ideas had to be tried, she urged her audience. She preferred young people who were willing to take risks on behalf of ideals. Conformism "will not get you into any trouble."

At a dinner to raise funds for the American Youth Congress in February 1939, Eleanor's impromptu remarks on the unfinished revolution that it seemed to her the New Deal represented led Heywood Broun to call her presentation "one of the finest short speeches in our times." The Republican speaker had belittled the NYA and CCC and, by implication, the WPA as ineffective and "mollycoddling," a favored epithet of the detractors. They were not "fundamental" answers, she replied thoughtfully, but "stopgaps" that gave desperate people hope and by which "we had bought ourselves time to think." New Deal measures "helped but they did not solve the fundamental problems. There is no use kidding ourselves. We have got to face this economic problem. And we have got to face it together." She delivered the simple words so that they seemed freighted with necessity, and indeed they have become a benchmark for historians writing about the period.

She befriended the Youth Congress leaders despite the presence of radicals, many of them Communists, in their ranks. She helped with their salaries, attended their weddings, and graced their meetings. When they descended upon the capital in "pilgrimages" or "institutes," as they called their massive lobbies, she opened Washington's many doors—and the White House—to them. She had long been persuaded that communism or socialism only succeeded as democracy failed. So she brushed aside the nay-sayers and admonishers in her own as well as her husband's entourages and embraced the discontented, welcoming their efforts to make democracy work for the ill-housed, ill-clothed, and ill-fed. Moreover, she liked the willingness of the Youth Congress leaders to stand by their positions when she had them to dinner at the White House with the president. She welcomed allies in her continuing argument with the president over where to draw the line between what was desirable and what was politically possible.

In 1957, in a recorded conversation with Arnold Michaelis, she hinted at the tensions between them engendered by this argument:

Mrs. Roosevelt: . . . I was not what you would call a 'yes man' because that wasn't what he needed.
Michaelis: But was that what he wanted?
Mrs. R.: I don't think it was what he wanted. I think, however, there were times . . . and particularly towards the end when he found argument very difficult, and even in the earlier days . . . he might have been happier if he had always been perfectly sure that I would have agreed. He wasn't and it was probably good for him that he wasn't. But there must have been times when he would have liked it if he didn't have to argue things.
M.: . . . Well you also said that sometimes you acted as a spur even though the spurring was not always wanted or welcome.
Mrs. R.: Yes, I think I did, very often because I had this horrible sense of obligation which was bred in me, I couldn't help it. It was nothing to be proud of, it was just something I couldn't help. And sometimes . . . Franklin had had, in a way, an easier life than I had had, and he hadn't had many difficulties. And sometimes he would like to do the easier thing, . . . And I think those were the times when he wished to goodness he didn't have

to look at someone who would demand of him what he really thought was the thing he ought to do. In a way, my conscience bothered him. And that's [a] perfectly natural thing. He was a very human person in a great many ways.

At the end of the thirties, with her strong sense of how much remained to be done, she was the one person around the president who did not join in the efforts to draft him for a third term. She did not consider it fitting for the president's wife to do so; moreover, it was the sort of decision that she felt, and Franklin insisted, he make on his own. She startled the author of this book at the beginning of 1940 when their friendship was beginning with the quiet observation the president might have served his purpose in history. Youth should not cling to him for leadership. New leadership was needed for the next step ahead. Unless, she added, the international crisis made him indispensable. In such circumstances only a person in whom the people had faith could be the stabilizing force.

She continued to hold this view through the spring of 1940 and the Nazi blitzkrieg. His running again, she told herself, might result in the same stalemate between the president and the Congress the country had witnessed since 1937. Her friends helped her reconcile herself to a third term. She believed sincerely that there were no indispensable leaders and had urged Franklin to prepare the way for a successor. An added impetus was her eagerness to get out of the goldfish bowl that life in the White House constituted.

A few months before Franklin decided to give the green light to the draft movement that he had supported, she let fall a revealing remark. She was curious, she said, whether Roy Howard of the Scripps-Howard papers would still want her column after she left the White House. She had deep doubts whether she was a leader in her own right, as her friends kept assuring her, but she was ready to test her ability to stand on her own away from the shadow of both Franklin and the White House.

8

PACIFISM
IS NOT ENOUGH

ELEANOR HAD RETURNED from her visit to Europe's battlefields, hospitals, and cemeteries after the first Great War infused with millennial hopes for the abolition of war. Although a faith in humanity impelled her in that direction, her actions always were seasoned with a sense for the practical. When she joined Esther Lape to promote the Bok peace prize contest in late 1923, she wrote, "Of course, we know that no formula, no plan, no one idea, no one mechanism of association among nations will immediately produce peace." A Wilsonian, she supported United States entry into the World Court as a feasible step toward the League of Nations, given America's opposition to "entanglements." She felt that women especially might be rallied for peace but cautioned them in her speeches to "grasp anything which is a step forward, not hold out for any particular ultimate panaceas." Nevertheless, women, with their intuition, tact, and feeling of "thoughtfulness for others in the daily affairs of life," were naturally disposed toward a better understanding of the troubles of other nations. If they resolved to find a substitute for war, wars would end, because "a woman's will is the strongest thing in the world." At the end of the twenties she was an internationalist and a gradualist. "None of us believe that the United States can disarm alone," she said in 1931. On entering the White House, she described herself as "a very realistic pacifist."

Franklin's willingness, however reluctant, in pursuit of election to renounce joining the League of Nations had so upset her that she did not speak to him for several days. But in view of her compact to stay at his side, she had no alternative but to reconcile herself to his sense of his political necessities. Once he was elected, however, she was after him anew to press for United States entry into the World Court. Both parties, after all, had had it in their platforms. In 1933 he told her the time was "politically unpropitious." But he did back entry at the beginning of 1935 when the Senate Foreign Relations Committee recommended it. As the resolution moved onto the floor of the Senate, a last-minute isolationist barrage prompted by William Randolph Hearst, the Reverend Charles E. Coughlin, and others inundated the Capitol. Esther Lape frantically appealed to her to go on the radio because they could get no man to do it. She spoke and hoped she did well, but the two-thirds needed in the Senate fell short of seven votes, she wrote Hick: "Enclosed is a copy of the useless speech. I rather expected the vote to go as it did. We are so prone to be led by the Hearsts & the Coughlins & the Longs & I am only really sorry that I pushed F.D.R. to try to pass it. Let us hope it doesn't imperil other things!"

She was a realist, but in accordance with her basic philosophy of helpfulness lent her support to some movements with which she did not fully agree as long as they were against war. At the request of Clarence Pickett, the director of the American Friends Service Committee, who worked with her at Arthurdale and who handled the funds she earned from speeches and writing, she supported the Quaker-sponsored Emergency Peace Campaign. In accordance with Quaker views it was pacifist and unilateralist, attitudes she did not share. "I think that all armament does cause distrust between nations," she agreed with Representative Jeannette Rankin, who would cast the lone vote against United States entry into World War II, "but that disarmament must be international so that no one country leaves itself open to attack or invasion from the other." To isolationist and pacifist arguments that the oceans were a sufficient protection to permit a greatly reduced navy, she replied. "The sea is no longer a real barrier between nations." When the same friends pointed to the prohibitive costs of military defenses, she replied that she wished "the money could be spent on other things," but, "Unless and until the strong nations of the world can agree to disarm, we must maintain our own forces; there is nothing else for us to do."

The strains on her marriage with Franklin were of sufficient sharpness to lead her during the 1936 campaign to say to a friend that yes, she knew FDR was a "great man" and "nice" to her, "but as a person, I'm a stranger & I don't want to be anything else." Nevertheless, in public matters they functioned as a team, and nowhere more so than in foreign affairs. In spite of political misgivings, he had yielded to her urgings and had tried to encourage United States entry into the World Court. In the short run, and politicians rarely think in other terms, he had been defeated, but in the long run it was a fight that had to be made, and that was her value to him. He, on his part, taught her—and through her a large section of the peace movement—that trust and love were inadequate as America's response to the world of dictators and militarists and that a preparedness program also had a place in a strategy for peace.

Sometimes they bent before the isolationist storms of the thirties, because they genuinely wanted the United States to keep out of war. He had his precinct captains, she had her peace cohorts. Both, however, were firmly internationalist. She favored economic sanctions against Mussolini's Italy because she hoped they might stop the invasion of Ethiopia. "Sanctions may be as bad as war," she wrote Carola von Schaeffer-Bernstein, a German roommate at Allenswood, now a supporter of Hitler, "but if they would stop the war quickly, I would agree that it was advisable to use them." The overthrow of the Weimar Republic had gladdened Carola, and she had accepted Hitler as the price of a resurgence of German nationalism. "Of course this country," Eleanor wrote her warningly, "still feels very much detached from the rest of the world because of its size and distance, but that will not last forever. I would like to see some methods for settling these differences adopted."

She was her husband's deputy within the peace movement arguing for realism. She was the peace movement's spokesman within the White House for its less millennarian demands. "Do encourage him to pursue it," Clarence Pickett wrote her after the president had floated the idea of a conference of "heads of nations" to try to reverse the surge toward war. "I think if reelected, he will put through something of the kind if he can get the agreement of the other heads," she replied.

She supported the Neutrality Act of 1935, which mandated the cutting off of all supplies to belligerent nations, aggressor nation and victim alike. Whatever hopes she had that it might help keep America out of war ebbed as Ethiopia, Spain, and China fell victim to fascist aggresstion. She favored the pacifist attitude of not seeking a fight; it was quite another thing, in her view, not to use one's power to prevent a fight. She wrote Elinor Morgenthau as reports of rearmament and repression poured out of Hitler's Germany and Mussolini was poised to invade Ethiopia:

*"She is perfect as a Queen," Mrs. Roosevelt wrote afterward, "gracious,
informed, saying the right thing and kind but a little self-consciously regal.*

Photographed by Edward Steichen

Mrs. Franklin D. Roosevelt in 1940. She permitted Steichen to take this formal photograph for Vogue.

She admired Madame Chiang Kai-shek. Her speech to Congress "marked the recognition of a woman who, through her own personality and her own service, has achieved a place in the world. . . ." January 1943

A portrait taken by Yousuf Karsh in Washington, D.C., 1944.

"The ladies' duties are all social and it would be boring except for the meals with a few people when the Prime Minister [Churchill] is entertaining. At the Citadel, Quebec, during the second Quebec conference. Left to right, H.R.H. Princess Alice, Winston Churchill, Eleanor Roosevelt, William L. Mackenzie King. September 1944

In 1949 with Mary McLeod Bethune. She was the fifteenth of seventeen children, some of whom had been sold into slavery. It was not until Mrs. Roosevelt had kissed Mrs. Bethune without thinking of it that she at last conquered the racial prejudice within herself.

She enjoyed arguments with her son John, the only Republican among her children. 1953

With Marshal Tito on Brionski Otoki, an island on the Adriatic. She thought he had a touch of greatness. 1953

She has her fortune told in Hong Kong. She did so occasionally, especially when with a friend whom it might amuse. 1955

Visiting a textile mill in the Soviet Union, 1957. "They love to keep you waiting, but they hate you to deviate from a plan you once made," she wrote about the Soviet travel bureau Intourist.

Receiving an honorary degree at Brandeis University, 1957. She envied those who were able to go to college.

At a press reception at the 1960 Democratic Convention in Los Angeles.

The children of Wiltwyck, a school for delinquent boys, picnic at Val-Kill. "400 hot dogs, 200 rolls, 200 cup cakes, 50 quarts of milk, 25 quarts of ice cream, 100 comics . . ." her card for annual occasions read. July 1959

She flew out to Minneapolis in 1961 to visit Elliott, who had recently remarried.

German news is horrible & I don't wonder you feel as you
do for I feel much the same. The Italian news too is dreadful & I feel keenly if we were in the League we might stop
this conflagration & if it starts even if we remain neutral we
will suffer in the end. It makes me sick.

The cause of Loyalist Spain underscored the fallacy of the mandatory arms embargo approach to world affairs, and she repeatedly
appealed to the president to seek its repeal. Few causes enlisted her
democratic sympathies as powerfully as did the Spanish Republic.
Golden-haired, Bryn Mawr-educated Martha Gellhorn, daughter of
a friend from League of Women Voter days and a writer of verve,
was an important source of information on the Iberian Republic.
Martha had reached Madrid, on whose outskirts Franco's armies had
been stopped, and then together with Ernest Hemingway had hurried back to the United States to work for the Loyalists. "We all listened to Martha Gellhorn while she told us of her experiences in
Spain," Eleanor wrote, describing a luncheon at the White House.

Eleanor had promoted *The Trouble I've Seen,* Martha's book of
stories based on her travels through America during the depression,
when Gellhorn served as an investigator for Harry Hopkins. She
had read aloud from it at the Colony Club and at Hyde Park. She
liked the way Martha placed her independence, ability, and good
looks at the service of the people. She arranged for Martha and
Ernest, who later married, to show the pro-Loyalist documentary,
The Spanish Earth, to her and the president. It was filmed by Joris
Ivens, a Dutch Communist. Hemingway wrote the narration. Both
Eleanor and the president wanted it made stronger.

As the "Devil's Decade," as one part of the thirties came to be
known, reached its boiling point, Eleanor moved from the peace
movement into the ranks of the anti-fascists. The aggressions of Hitler, Mussolini, and the Japanese militarists dispelled her sympathies
for their countries as "have-not" nations and the "victims" of unfair
treaties. Fascist militarism, racial incitements, invasions, and bombing of open cities altered her views about the use of force. "I have
never believed that war settled anything satisfactorily," she wrote at
the end of 1937 after low-flying Japanese bombers attacked and sank
the United States gunboat *Panay* in Chinese waters. ". . . a country is
worse off when it does not go to war for its principles than if it went
to war."

Strongly anti-fascist, she was no ideologue. Amid the passions let loose by the Spanish war, a small episode demonstrated the primacy of her feeling for human beings. Children had been evacuated from the Basque strongholds in northern Spain, having been taken through fascist lines to safety zones, a humanitarian gesture that the State Department, urged by Eleanor, had persuaded Franco to make. Loyalist friends wanted to bring 500 of these children to the United States, partly because it was a safe refuge but also because of their propaganda value. It needed more than emotion to do the wise thing, she advised Martha. It was fairer to the children and their parents to keep them as near Spain as possible. How not react emotionally, Martha wrote in self defense, in the face of Franco's indiscriminate bombing of Madrid and Bilbao? Eleanor conceded her right to feel emotional. "I simply meant that in our feelings towards the children we must not let our best judgment be warped by our emotions." When the editor of the Catholic diocesan paper *The Tablet,* hoping to embarrass her, asked whether the proceeds of a milk fund to aid the "distressed children" of Spain that listed her as a sponsor were to be used for children in Nationalist as well as Loyalist territory, she replied, "I make no distinction in children. Any needing help should be helped."

As her advocacy of the Loyalist cause became more outspoken and militant, the Catholic hierarchy intensified its attacks on her. They did not deter her from defiantly defending the Americans who had fought in the Abraham Lincoln Brigade, many of them Communists. "I am not neutral in feeling, as I believe in Democracy and the right of a people to choose their own government without having it imposed on them by Hitler and Mussolini."

But she was unable to persuade Franklin either to urge Congress to repeal the embargo on Republican Spain or to do it by executive action, as many lawyers, including Henry L. Stimson, believed he had the power to do. The country still felt that the arms embargo helped to keep the United States out of foreign entanglements. He was intent, moreover, on keeping his position aligned with Great Britain and France, and they were responsible for the League's policy of nonintervention. He was deterred too by the threat of a falling away in the Catholic vote, which had been strongly New Deal.

"[W]e had better build our own fires to counteract their [pro-Nationalist] pressures," she advised the columnist Max Lerner, who informed her he would have to attack the president sharply on the embargo issue. She was even more outspoken at a White House dinner attended by Leon Henderson, a militant New Dealer and Loyalist supporter, after Franco's victory. "You and I, Mr. Henderson, will some day learn a lesson from the tragic error over Spain. We were morally right, but too weak." She looked at the president as if he were not there. "We should have pushed *him* harder."

Throughout the thirties she had urged the need to deal with problems "before they reach the point where people will want to go to war about them. . . . I don't think leadership lies along the path of isolation." Implicit in her approach to the world's affairs was the acceptance of responsibilities, not in her case because of the ordinary rewards such as power, wealth, and privilege, but because duty and usefulness to others were bred into her being. They fed her sense of human solidarity. Others might speak of balances of power; she saw human beings.

Spain reinforced her view that the United States was unable to escape war once it broke out. "That is something which I have preached from coast to coast on deaf ears I fear. We are all of us selfish . . . nobody can save his skin alone. We must all hang together." She still recoiled from the prospect of war. She did not agree with Thomas Mann, the great German novelist who had taken refuge in the United States and who felt that "force must be met with force," for "that is what we have been doing from generation to generation." And if there was a war, what was the United States, what was she prepared to do? She joined in the worldwide sigh of relief when Munich for a moment seemed to lift the likelihood of war, although she was sorry for "the poor Zchecks! *[sic]*. . . . I don't somehow like the role of England and France, do you?" she asked Franklin. "We can say nothing however for we wouldn't go to war for someone else"

The uprush of wars and dictatorships produced refugees who begged to come to the United States. But revulsion to what was happening abroad intensified xenophobia within the United States. Its doors of admission were sealed more tightly. In vain did Roosevelt chide the Daughters of the American Revolution with the reminder that we were all children of immigrants. "What has happened to us in this country?" Eleanor repeatedly asked. With Franklin's consent and advice in 1939 she supported the introduction of a bipartisan bill to admit 10,000 children a year for two years in excess of the German quota in order to make it easier for Germany's Jews to escape Hitler's genocidal mania. Restrictionist groups led by the patriotic societies inundated the hearings; the president reluctantly wrote "File No Action" and Senator Robert Wagner reluctantly withdrew his

Child Refugee Bill lest existing quotas be cut, a realistic acceptance of realities that later generations have unfairly ascribed to FDR's indifference.

"We used to be more sensitive to human need," Eleanor grieved. Once she had accepted the racial stereotypes of the society in which she had been reared, but by the end of the thirties she saw such prejudices—and at the moment Jews were the special target—as reflections of insecurity and envy. "When a person holds deep prejudice," she had grown to realize, "he gets to dislike the object of his prejudice. He uses it as an excuse of something unworthy in himself." If a minority had disagreeable mannerisms—the Jews, for example, clannishness, of which she considered Zionism an extreme form—that was the result of what a dominant society had done to them. She sought out those whom society shunned, ignoring cries of "Jew-lover," and "Nigger-lover." When in 1940 she heard that Isabella Greenway, one of her bridesmaids and a lifelong friend, had come out for Wendell Willkie, she observed mildly that "with her new husband she could scarcely do otherwise," but when she subsequently heard that one of Isabella's reasons for doing so was that Franklin was too much under the influence of the Jews, she hoped it was not true. If it was, she could not bring herself to speak to Isabella again.

The fascist press denounced her as a "bad influence" on her husband, but he needed no lessons from anyone in his efforts to get the neutrality laws amended so that America's power short of war might be used to aid the democracies and to further the cause of human solidarity.

He was the impresario on the occasion of the state visit of King George VI and Queen Elizabeth, organizing it as an unspoken demonstration to Hitler in the summer of 1939 of what America's isolationism kept him from saying out loud—that in a showdown the democracies would stick together. Although he supervised every detail of protocol, ceremony, and program, the visit also bore Eleanor's special stamp and showed the king and queen a distinctive face of America—the New Deal reforms, Marian Anderson, the folk singer Allen Lomax, Kate Smith, even hot dogs. There was Eleanor, wrote a kinswoman in her diary, "dashing about . . . just as though it were only a family party." As the Roosevelts and some of their Hyde Park neighbors bade the royal couple goodbye and the train pulled away from the Hyde Park station, all broke into "Auld Lang Syne." Eleanor captured the mood of the moment. "We all knew the King and Queen were returning home to face a war."

"... [O]ur hands, as far as prevention goes, are pretty well tied," she wrote after the Senate Foreign Relations Committee refused to end the mandatory arms embargo provision of the neutrality laws. A few weeks later Hitler secured himself against a two-front war by signing a pact with Stalin. War still seemed to her a dreadful alternative. She quoted a line to Franklin that she had read: "War is nothing but an escape from the problems of peace."

Then it came. "At five o'clock this morning our telephone rang," she reported in *My Day*, from Hyde Park, "and it was my husband in Washington to tell me the sad news that Germany had invaded Poland. ..." She had just received a letter from Carola written August 19 begging her to try to see Germany's view. Her draft reply, which she sent to Sumner Welles to review, leaned over backwards in order to dispose her erstwhile school friend to give her a hearing. "... [t]here may be a need for curtailing the ascendancy of the Jewish people," her reply read, but it might have been done in a more humane way. She concluded, "I hope we are not facing another four years of struggle and I hope that our country will not go to war, but no country can exist free and unoppressed while a man like Hitler remains in power." And to a conscientious objector she wrote that she would "rather die than submit to rule by Hitler and Stalin, would not you?"

9

1940

IT IS ALWAYS DIFFICULT to correlate a person's emotional and private life with his or her public life. It is almost impossible in the case of a musician, poet, or mathematician but hazardous too with a charismatic figure like Eleanor Roosevelt, in whom saintliness was joined to practical wisdom, hopefulness with a resigned sense that "all is vanity," piety toward the past with an openness to the new. She was a woman of bewildering paradox and density of feeling. These were often made inaccessible by the depressions to which she occasionally succumbed and kept concealed until her ruling perception that "life was meant to be lived" returned to save her. One has to chart her development between the wars through her writings and her choice of friends who helped her find a path toward self-realization. Fortunately, she was, as her son said, one of the "writingest ladies" of our times, especially to her close friends.

All accepted her and Franklin's decision to stay together even as they helped her shape an existence on her own. The list of people in the twenties and thirties begins with Louis Howe and included Nancy Cook, Marion Dickerman, Elinor Morgenthau, Earl Miller, Esther Lape, Elizabeth Read, Malvina Thompson, Lorena Hickok, and, at the end of the thirties, the author of this book. Just as Louis had helped her, indeed had pushed her, into politics at the beginning of the twenties, and Lorena Hickok had reconciled her to her role as first lady, so her friendship with the author sustained her in the crisis of 1940—a crisis occasioned by Franklin's decision to run for a third term, the outbreak of the dreaded war in Europe, and her disenchantment with the leaders in the American Youth Congress.

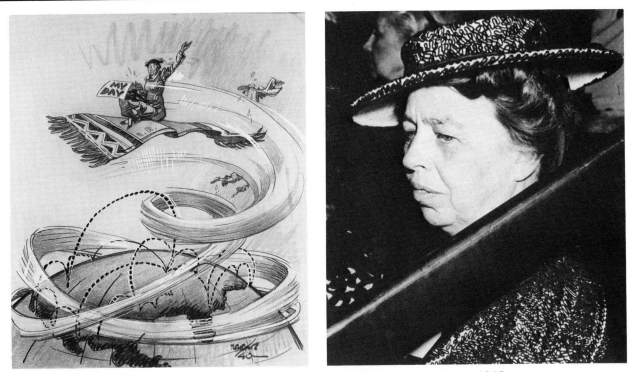

TOP LEFT: *"Speaking of migrants" cartoon in the* San Francisco News, *1940.* TOP RIGHT: *Eleanor listens to FDR in the gallery of the House of Representatives, May 16, 1940. Hitler's armies had overrun the Low Countries and were plunging through France. Franklin had made similar defense-related requests before today, she noted, "and the reasons that he can get them today is that circumstances hit the people of the United States in the head."* BOTTOM: *She receives 6,000 women party workers of the Women's Division of the Democratic National Committee in May 1940.*

In the Monroe Room of the White House beneath a portrait of her grandfather.

"Don't let her down; it will break her heart," Aubrey Williams, the spirited leader of the National Youth Administration, adjured the American Youth Congress leaders after Eleanor had appeared at the hearings of the House Committee on Un-American Activities and thereby indicated her support of the young people appearing before it. Williams, a southerner, was a man of verve and vision, and not lacking in courage.

A phenomenon of the late thirties was the proliferation of "Popular Front" organizations. They brought together radicals, liberals, even a few conservatives in support of such causes as aid to Spain, civil rights, collective security, the young. Public-spirited and anti-fascist, Eleanor backed several of these groups. The Communists—because it suited the purposes of the Soviet Union, which was then in fear of Hitler and needed allies in the West—were in these organizations, often as founders, sometimes as colonizers. Liberals and intellectuals regarded the Soviet Union hopefully and the Communists in their midst sympathetically.

Eleanor was among the latter. She understood the conditions that bred Communists, was not surprised or discomfited to find them active in groups committed to the eradication of poverty and war, and was convinced they found a hearing only to the extent that democratic society failed to meet human needs. All went well until the Hitler-Stalin pact in August 1939, which outraged the liberals and shocked even the Communists. But equally disturbing to people of good will was the way many of their erstwhile friends in these organizations overnight became foes of aid to England and France in a war that the pact had unleashed and also advocates of a "third party" instead of a "third term," of which they had been strenuous promoters.

Eleanor, who was deeply patriotic, with a strong awareness of the contribution her forebears had made in the building of America, and profoundly democratic in her outlook, considered loyalty to a foreign power that was ruled by a dictator repellant and alien. She found herself in battles everywhere, against the Communists who sought to control the American Newspaper Guild and against their domination of Spanish aid activities and their efforts to take over the Workers Alliance, the organization of the unemployed. In some cases she tried to save the organization by her support of the non-Communists in it, in others she shifted her support to organizations that served the same purposes.

Her most difficult disentanglement was with the American Youth Congress, to whose leaders she had given her heart as well as her support. The friendships that had begun in the mid-thirties reached their climax when she threw all her efforts and prestige into opening Washington's doors to the American Youth Congress "citizenship institute," as its lobbying effort was called, even persuading the president to address it from the portico at the rear of the White House.

February 1940 was an ambiguous moment in the Youth Congress leadership's affairs. It was moving from collective security ("war anywhere is war everywhere") to "the Yanks are not coming" phase yet did not want to lose the patronage and friendship of the first lady. But the duty to support Soviet Russia's invasion of Finland, or at least to keep silent about it, made an equivocal position more difficult. Several thousand young paraders stood in the rain on the White House lawn and heard FDR denounce as "unadultered twaddle" Youth Congress claims that a loan to Finland was an attempt to force the United States into an imperalistic war. Some booed and many of the nation's editorialists applauded the president's spanking of the ill-mannered dissenters. It was a speech he seems to have written himself, perhaps because it was addressed as much to his wife as to the Youth Congress and the nation. There were, of course, "strange reticences" between the two, as Jonathan Daniels, who was devoted to them both, once said. But there is no other evidence that he ever sought to deter her from her advocacy of the Youth Congress or other "popular front" groups. She remarked about the American Youth Act, a billion-dollar bill introduced by the American Youth Congress to aid chiefly the young people who were out of school and out of work, "I don't think it will pass, but I think it may get us a little more money for NYA. . . ." That was his purpose too.

The Youth Congress leaders had been staunch allies in Eleanor's running argument with the president to lighten the hand of the Army in the Civilian Conservation Corps and to strengthen the NYA. Indeed, during his third term, as conscription and the defense buildup altered America's manpower needs, he gave orders to his bill drafters to prepare legislation to combine the NYA and CCC into a single agency and place it on a standby basis, a position with which she concurred. Both foresaw that after the war, the problem of jobless youth would still disquiet the country.

As for the leaders of the Youth Congress whom she had personally befriended, when they came to her after Hitler's invasion of Soviet Russia in June 1941 and proposed they resume cooperation, she rebuffed their overture: "You have forgotten conversations all of you had with me in the summer of 1940, and therefore do not realize the effect . . . the changed position you had taken since the invasion of Russia has had on me." She refused to work with them politically, but if they should get into trouble personally she was ready to help them as individuals. She was a woman of mercy right out of the First Corinthians. That was her favorite New Testament passage. "And now abideth faith, hope, charity, these three; but the greatest of these is charity."

The reluctance with which she dissociated herself from the Youth Congress paralleled the evolution of her attitude toward the war that broke out in September 1939. She and Franklin had "four sons just of the age to go to war." "I imagine I know much more about what it means than most of you do," she told her Youth Congress auditors; "because I was very close to it in the last World War, and I do not want to see this country go to war again." But her anti-war sentiments had not curbed her anti-fascism in the thirties, and when Youth Congress leaders challenged the real purpose of the nation's support for Finland in light of its indifference to other victims of aggression, she replied, "I agree with you that a stand should have been taken when Ethopia was attacked. I agree with you in your sympathy for Spain. I agree with you in your sympathy for China and Czechoslovakia, but I also have sympathy for Finland."

She supported the Burke-Wadsworth conscription bill in the summer of 1940 but wanted it geared with the NYA / CCC and kept from being exclusively administered by the army. She favored the training of young women as well as men, just as she supported military preparedness and believed that the defense program should serve the purposes of community revitalization. Others focused on immediate defense needs, which they saw as purely military; she was constantly looking for the key to the public's conscience that might again dispose it as it had in 1933 to think of their neighbors' happiness as well as their own. She was a firm advocate of aid to Britain, including the destroyer-for-bases deal that the president and Winston Churchill announced at the end of the 1940 summer, and followed closely the reports of new thinking in England even among its Conservatives that emerged after the fall of France.

Though she took part in Franklin's third-term campaign only reluctantly because she was so unhappy over the prospect of another four years in the White House, she performed one indispensable service. In July 1940, when a restive Democratic national convention

After clearing it with Franklin, she flew out to the Democratic Convention in Chicago. The atmosphere was "deadly." James Farley, the Democratic National Chairman, and Franklin Jr. greeted her on arrival.

after drafting the president for a third term balked over his selection of Henry Wallace as his running mate, she flew out to Chicago. She did so at the request of Frances Perkins, who said the atmosphere at the convention was "deadly," and only after she had Franklin's concurrence, for she was punctiliously careful not to encroach on his prerogatives. He would not countenance "petticoat rule," and neither would the public. In a few remarks at the convention she managed to dispel the miasma of rancor and jobbery that hung over it and pave the way for Wallace's nomination. "You will have to rise above considerations which are narrow and partisan. This is a time when it is the United States we fight for," she implored.

"You turned a rout into a victory," the dean of American progressives, Senator George Norris, wrote her. "That victory was finally

"Mrs. Roosevelt Stills the Tumult of 50,000," a headline read. "You will have to rise above considerations which are narrow and partisan," she said. "This is a time when it is the United States we fight for." The roll call began; she had saved the day for Wallace.

realized is due, in my opinion, more to you than to any other one thing. That one act makes you heroic."

She had always declined to campaign for her husband except to appear at his campaign rallies. Nineteen-forty was no exception. But a quiet footnote in her column showed that she was that rare person in political life who did not make promises that might be unfulfillable. In the closing days of the campaign, Republican orators pounded the theme that Roosevelt would get the country into the war. FDR yielded to his political advisors and in Boston assured America's "mothers and fathers [that] your boys are not going to be sent into any foreign wars." Eleanor's column afterwards sounded a caveat. "No one can honestly promise you today peace at home or abroad. All any human being can do is to promise that he will do his utmost to prevent this country being involved in war."

On election night at Hyde Park after the returns showed that Roosevelt had been reelected, she went in to say goodnight to him, to be met with the startling comment, "We seem to have averted a putsch." Perhaps she had been selfish, she said to this author afterwards, and wanting to get out of the White House had tended to underestimate the importance of the president's reelection.

10

REFORM
THROUGH
DEFENSE

You have certainly left golden footprints behind you.
—WINSTON CHURCHILL

In 1940 the first full-length biography of Eleanor appeared, a measure of how much she had touched the public's awareness. *Eleanor Roosevelt,* by Ruby Black, one of the reporters who had covered her press conferences, adequately covered her life as a "personage," although only half of that, for Eleanor was fifty-six and would live another twenty-two very full years. But it only brushed the "person," for little was known about the private side of her life, and for her an intense private life was indispensable to effective public functioning. So she began her third term as first lady.

Yet the nation also knew her, better perhaps than most public figures, not only through *This Is My Story,* the first volume of her autobiography, but also through "My Day"; the monthly question-and-answer page in a woman's magazine that startled readers with the candor and crispness of her replies; her regular appearances on radio networks; her endless travels through America; and innumerable speeches.

Her four strapping sons were called to active duty in 1941—a wrenching event, for the odds were slight that all would return. She wrote a friend, "No matter what one's children are, one never loses the feeling, at least I can't, that they are mine, part of me, as they were when they were little and helpless in my arms and I love them dearly."

Mama died in 1941. The president's sorrow over her death went

Driving to Town Hall in Hyde Park to vote, November 5, 1940.

At the Third Inaugural Party, January 19, 1941. Eleanor with (left to right) Sara Delano Roosevelt, Mrs. Elliott Roosevelt, Captain Elliott Roosevelt, and Captain James Roosevelt.

At her desk in the White House with Malvina Thompson (left) and Edith B. Helm, her social secretary.

deep, for he was devoted to his mother as she had been to him, but there was little outward expression of his grief. He kept his emotions to himself, whereas Eleanor had to express what she felt. "Mama had a wonderful end," she wrote her aunt, but noted in another letter that "It is dreadful to have lived so close to someone for 36 years and feel no deep affection or sense of loss. It is hard on Franklin however." "She attended to everything," noted a cousin about Eleanor and Sara's death. The death of her younger brother Hall of cirrhosis of the liver a few weeks later was a more anguished event. For ten days she kept vigil at his bedside in the hospital, sleeping in her clothes. "My idea of hell, if I believed in it, would be to sit or stand and watch someone breathing hard, strugging for words when a gleam of consciousness returns and thinking 'this was once the little boy I played with and scolded, he could have been so much and this is what he is.'" The contrast in the way she and Franklin reacted to the deaths in the family reflected the two temperaments—one craved and gave intimacy, the other hid his most private thoughts and feelings.

As always she transcended grief through immersion in work.

Eleanor is sworn in as assistant director of the office of Civilian Defense, September 29, 1941. With New York Mayor Fiorella La-Guardia, the director. She was in charge of volunteer participation and community organization.

The closer the United States moved toward war, the more she wanted to play a part in the nation's mobilization. She had definite, highly personal views on social reform through wartime mobilization. The latter should be total, include women, and, through defense-related services such as health and child care, nutrition, housing, training, and education, revitalize the nation's communities. What a conservative Congress begrudged when presented under the rubric of social reform, it might accept as social defense. So she accepted the president's designation of her as co-director of the Office of Civilian Defense (OCD), though she had misgivings. As wife of the president she both carried greater authority than the ordinary official and became the target of those who feared to attack him directly, especially after Pearl Harbor, which had united the nation. She and Mayor LaGuardia, her co-director, flew out to the West Coast, whose cities were blacked out amid reports of Japanese bombings. "[I]t does seem to calm people down," she said of her presence afterward.

The spotlight of national attention was unsparing. Another official might have worked in relative obscurity at the programs of physical fitness, nutrition, and literacy by which Eleanor sought to build up social standards, but her leadership was denounced as an effort to "socialize America." The attacks on her were savage. Though she assured one and all, "Please don't be disturbed, I love a fight," in February 1942 she decided to resign in the hopes of saving the volunteer participation program. "To know me is a terrible thing," she explained, as friends whom she had enlisted in the program were attacked. She realized that in some respects it was unwise for "a vulnerable person like myself to try a government job," but she never doubted that the attack on her was "purely political and made by the same people who have fought NYA, CCC, WPA, Farm Security, etc."

The OCD experience upset and saddened her, but she soon was in search of other chances to be of use in the war effort. She was particularly solicitous of the men and women in the armed forces. "The boys are certainly doing some talking and thinking," she said hopefully after a cross-country flight on which the other passengers were ferry pilots, but afterward wrote Franklin, "I am finding it harder and harder to talk to these groups of boys. We spend now to send them to die for a 'way of life,' and a few years ago the very men who spend so willingly and speed them on their way were afraid of taxes to make this same way of life give them a chance to earn a living." Another letter asked, "Will we do it all over again when those that live through it come back with McKellars and Byrds [reactionary senators] in power?" Her faith was in the young. "This generation is

With GIs on the White House lawn, June 12, 1942.

much more serious than the 1918 army was in regards the future," she wrote her aunt Maude, then in Dublin.

There were changes in the White House. In July 1942 Harry Hopkins, whose access to Franklin she had facilitated, married Louise Macy, who had charm and an ability to please men that Eleanor had never been able to achieve. Harry's unwillingness, after he had moved into the White House, to be her confederate as well as Franklin's, as Louis Howe had been, had proved a wrenching experience. The White House was divided between president and first lady, Harry once explained, and both demanded absolute loyalty. It was not only a disenchantment with Harry that shadowed her relationship with Louise. She brooked no competition as mistress of the White House. "[W]e ought to manage to get on," she wrote drily when she heard that Franklin wanted Harry and Louise to try living at the White House. The very tentativeness of her statement suggested her doubts.

Harry and Louise decided, however, to Eleanor's satisfaction, that they preferred living in their own house after marrying.

In the fall Franklin decided that a state visit by Eleanor to Great Britain would serve a useful purpose. Accompanied by Tommy, she flew to England, to be met when she reached bomb-ravaged London by the king and queen, with whom she was driven to Buckingham Palace. She visited troops in the rain, slogged through the mud to inspect volunteer services, spent a weekend at Chequers with Prime Minister Churchill, argued with him over Loyalist Spain, stopped with dowager Queen Mary at Beaufort Castle—"not a hilarious meal"—and made endless speeches, including one over the facilities of the BBC and another to the London County Council. As she departed, Churchill sent her a note saying, "You have certainly left golden footprints behind you." As the homeward plane taxied to a halt in Washington, "we looked out and saw several Secret Service men and several cars and knew that FDR had taken time to meet us. . . . I really think Franklin was glad to see me back. . . ." She wanted to do well for him; she wanted to be missed.

"I have been so busy since I came home, I haven't had time to

Eleanor is met at Paddington Station in bomb-ravaged London by the king and queen. October 23, 1942.

107

With the royal family in Buckingham Palace, October 24. The future Queen Elizabeth sits on the arm of the chair, Princess Margaret below her.

breathe," she told an old friend a few weeks later, and yet to another she also confided, "I'm alone inside so much. . . ." One way of keeping sadness at bay was achieving a "sense of 'oneness' with people one loves. . . ." That was what made love "important to the person that gives it." Another way was to hold steady before one's eyes the desire to make this a better world, to ensure that the war was not being fought in vain. As Allied troops, some of which she had inspected while in England, liberated North Africa, she argued with Franklin against the return of fascist governments anywhere. She also sounded out Franklin on being allowed to go to China and Russia. Her consciousness of the color issue had been heightened by the war. She was among the nation's chief white protagonists of racial

In London.

A shelter in the caves under the White Cliffs of Dover.

equality and shared Pearl S. Buck's awareness after Pearl Harbor that more basic than Chinese antagonism to Japan might be the colored races' antagonism toward the white. "The whole world is faced with the same situation," Eleanor warned, "the domination of the white race is being challenged." It was part and parcel of the same fight going on within the country. "Unless we make the country worth fighting for by Negroes," she replied to a critic of her racial views in the United States, "we would have nothing to offer the world at the end of the war."

She pushed the president and Hopkins to the point of exasperation because she felt that a Negro tenant farmer who had been sentenced to death for the murder of a landlord by a jury of landlords from which Negroes had been excluded had become the symbol of a racially stacked system. When race riots swept Detroit, some blamed them on her, and she was advised not to visit the city. Blacks had to be part of a truly democratic consensus, and even though it made her the target in the South of the forces that were trying to break FDR's hold over the region, she persisted in her advocacy.

"We must trust the people, that is the first lesson," she wrote after seeing *The Patriots,* a play about Thomas Jefferson. A few weeks later, the same thought had an international dimension. "Only if we trust and believe others' good intentions," the "others" meaning Soviet Russia and China, "can they be expected to believe in ours. We can't be the only trustworthy people in the world." Henry Wallace's "Century of the Common Man" speech exhilarated her. She shared his faith in the common man. She had heard the president and prime minister speak of a British-American condominium to run the postwar world and was relieved to hear her husband later broaden the concept to include the Chinese and the Russians. "I do not think this is an American century," she wrote a former aid at the OCD; "I like Henry Wallace's 'people's century' better." The war had to be fought as "a people's war" or there was "a grave danger that it will be followed by a peace which is not a people's peace."

When the slim, American-educated Madame Chiang Kai-shek arrived at the White House in early 1943 as the emissary of the generalissimo, Eleanor was among those in the capital who took to her. She "could not help a great feeling of pride in her as a woman but when she spoke [to a joint session of Congress it was no longer as a woman that one thought of her." She "has already asked FDR if I can go back with her," a private letter said. After a while she noted that Madame's talk of democracy contrasted disturbingly with her imperious ways. It did not, however, diminish her hope of going

On her trip to the Southwest Pacific, August 17 through September 23, 1943. "[E]very man who fights for us is in some way, our man . . . and if your heart is with any man, in some way it must be with all," she said at the end of her trip.

Guadalcanal inspection. "I was ashamed of my original surliness," wrote Admiral Halsey, who had not wanted her to go to an area that was still being bombed. She alone had accomplished more good "than any other person who had passed through the area," he added.

to China and perhaps even to Russia, for Stalin's chief lieutenant, V. M. Molotov, had asked her to do so when he came to Washington as "Mr. Brown." In the end the president ruled out trips either to China or Russia. He hoped himself to meet Stalin and Chiang "and wants to wait on that." Instead he suggested she visit American troops in the South Pacific and New Zealand and Australia. As usual misgivings beset her. The trip might be assailed as a political gesture, but she decided finally she should go in the hopes especially that she might make American soldiers "feel that Franklin wants to know about them."

She flew to the South Pacific in a four-engined Army Liberator. The beginning of the trip was shadowed by discontent because the admirals and generals were unwilling to let her approach any of the "danger spots" such as Guadalcanal in the Solomons and Port Moresby off Australia. But she went about her job resolutely, walked through "miles" (wrote Admiral Halsey), of hospitals, going into every ward, stopping at every bed, speaking to every patient. In New Zealand she visited war factories, Red Cross Clubs, and troops as well as Maoris and government officials. In Australia, "General MacArthur was too busy to bother with a lady," she jibed, and to Franklin she complained: "I have an MP escort everywhere that would do you credit. I have all the pomp and restriction and none of the power! I'm coming home this time and go in a factory!"

She did get to Guadalcanal on her return to Noumea after Australia. "I was ashamed of my original surliness," Admiral Halsey later wrote. By the trip's end she had covered seventeen islands, New Zealand, and Australia and seen about 400,000 men in camps and hospitals. She left the South Pacific with "a sense of pride in the young people of this generation which I can never express and a sense of obligation which I feel I can never discharge." Her conscience permitted no rest, for how was it possible to look in the eyes of the boys she had seen in the hospitals, if one did not try to make this a more decent world? But she had to defer to the president. Churchill at Harvard had suggested a common Anglo-American citizenship, and she worried with Henry Wallace that the prime minister was pushing for a United States-British alliance—"and we believed in a United Nations one. We thought that Franklin did but it might not yet be the moment to shout about it. . . . So I asked FDR and gathered he would like us all to keep quiet."

Within the privacy of the family, however, she pressed for a United Nations approach. She had to move more gingerly than ever, for Franklin was beginning to wear out. He began to ail. In the prep-

TOP: *Eleanor greets her Maori guide, Rangi, in Rotorua, New Zealand, August 31.* BOTTOM: *Messing at the navy base hospital at Efate, New Hebrides.*

arations for the UN Relief and Rehabilitation Conference, his food message to Congress contained much that she had advocated but thought he had never accepted. That was his way, she told a very few friends afterward. He fought her, teased her, ignored her, all the while picking her brain and being guided by her conscience. But he was becoming less patient, and though he liked to have members of his family with him when he went to his meetings with Churchill, Stalin, and Chiang, he found reasons not to have her along.

In March he sent her on the third of her wartime trips, this one to visit United States stations in the Caribbean and Latin America. She was talking with *"officers* and *men,"* she wrote Franklin, and though she performed her job staunchly she had a sense of being away from where things were happening. Franklin had to keep the conservatives in Congress with him to fight the war; she feared a hollow peace. He portrayed himself at the beginning of 1944 as "Dr. Win-the-War" and said that "Old Dr. New Deal's remedies had been for internal troubles." She made a rare public dissent. She was not ready to lay the New Deal "away in lavender." And if it were to be dropped as a goal, the country needed something more in its place than "win-the-war."

Toward the end of her journey through the Caribbean, Franklin had gone to Bernard Baruch's plantation in South Carolina to recover from "the flu." No one told her that one of his visitors there was the widowed Mrs. Rutherfurd, Lucy Mercer. One can only surmise her reaction had she known. When she had accepted to stay at his side at the end of World War I, he had agreed not to see Lucy again. Perhaps she was foolish, as Hall's first wife said after her death, to believe such a promise. In 1944, moreover, both Franklin and Lucy were relatively elderly, and their unmistakable pleasure in each other's company was that of a remembered romance. That made it more striking that Eleanor was not told. Some kept their silence because of their respect for this woman of dignity, a few because they feared to rekindle her sense of having failed as a woman.

At the end of March, Franklin's ailments were finally diagnosed by a young heart specialist, Dr. Howard G. Bruenn, a naval lieutenant whom Admiral McIntire, the White House physician, should have brought in earlier, as "hypertension, hypertensive heart disease, cardiac failure (left ventricular) and acute bronchitis." Eleanor, so far as is known, was not aware he had congestive heart failure, and hypertension seems to have had little meaning for her, but she did know that he tired very easily and had little "pep," as she put it. She also had the impression that he needed her more. She was resigned in the summer of 1944 to trying to live in the big house at Hyde Park and to keep it "really pleasant. Never from choice would I live here and never alone." Franklin's son James said his father needed "a touch of triviality" to ease burdens his mother was unable to provide despite her strength and almost saintly selflessness. She went about her business doing what she was allowed to do, unknowing about Lucy, while Franklin and those about him eager to shield her from hurt kept the truth from her.

As a result of her marriage to Franklin, she had become the most celebrated woman of her time; and though as first lady, to paraphrase the poet John Ashbery, she had fought becoming a prisoner of her own fame, she had not succeeded in playing a pivotal role in the world's affairs. The latter in part was Franklin's doing. He had to be the center of attention, would not tolerate rivalry; moreover, the world still regarded war and politics as man's business.

The Allies moved closer to victory, and postwar planning intensified. She pushed for the inclusion of women in such meetings and presided over a White House conference on "How Women May Share" in postwar policy making. She conferred regularly with Bernard Baruch, whose recommendations to Congress on "War and Postwar Adjustment Policies" asked the right questions and whom she brought together with young labor leaders like James Carey and Walter Reuther. She was pleased to give the latter, on his way toward becoming president of the United Automobile Workers, a chance "to work on" Baruch, because like Reuther she feared that reconversion might not have full employment as one of its goals. She also pressed for a more sympathetic attitude by her husband's advisors toward the wily old financier.

The need for jobs at home was at the forefront of her thinking about the future, yet in almost prophetic fashion she foresaw that domestic well-being was bound up with the stability of the international economic order that would emerge from the war. The first requisite of such an order was the alleviation of hunger in the world, but second was that nations everywhere should be able to build their economies "on a scale of plentiful production in order that there may be full employment for all people and a rising standard of living throughout the world." That theme had been part of her message in the South Pacific. She had conveyed to American troops Franklin's greetings and appealed to the home front to provide jobs for the returning men. To New Zealanders and Australians she presaged an international economic truth that became clearer to Amer-

115

icans in the 1980s when the stability of the international economic arrangements moved to the forefront of the world's agenda. The time had come "for world thinking," she urged everywhere. Economies "of abundance and employment" were needed by all "with low prices on goods so that people who are just beginning to struggle upwards in the rest of the world and who need our goods will be able to buy them." The Western nations needed "world markets," and "we must try to help the people to whom we wish to sell, and to produce such things as we wish to buy because a one-sided economy is never in the long run, of permanent value."

Vice President Henry Wallace was the political leader whose thinking about worldwide Tennessee Valley Authority (TVA) and WPA projects, as well as colonialism, approximated her own. She urged Franklin to retain him as his running mate in 1944, but Franklin excluded her, as he had usually done, from the crucial conferences with his political lieutenants where the decision was made to drop Wallace from the ticket. She had questions about the vice president's political wisdom—"he's not a good politician," she wrote a friend—but as the 1944 convention neared, she wrote a column favoring his renomination, "but Franklin says I must hold it till after the convention." Then she added words that spoke a volume about the restrictions on her as first lady: "I wish I were free."

Eleanor Roosevelt was no theoretical thinker. Indeed, she was always slightly in awe of those who were and lamented her lack of college training. But few people in public life exceeded the grasp and sympathy with which she approached ideas that were presented to her. She saw the world with the eyes and curiosity of a young person and refused to be cowed by ideological systems. The laws proclaimed by economists, sociologists, and theologians were human artifacts and as such amenable to human effort. When she said "life must be lived with adventurous courage" she had in mind resistance not only to the blows of fate but to the pronouncements of the theorists. Sometimes her thinking had verged on the chiliastic but her immersion in the world's realities—and Franklin—had always been there to pull her back.

She was resigned to her fate in 1944. "I dread another campaign and even more another 4 years in Washington but since he's running for the good of the country I hope he wins." Both Republican and Democratic platforms in 1944 were full of promises. "All one should say is: 'Build a character that can meet new conditions without fear, develop the power to think things thro' and face facts and recognize the interdependence among men." Although she

shrank from another four years in the White House, she approved
of Franklin's decision to run and to pay the price of doing so. In
Quebec with the president for a meeting with Churchill, she hoped
"for the sake of these negotiations and the future, that Franklin is
elected and continues vigorous in the future."

She did not campaign for Franklin. But she was outspoken about
the issues in the campaign, which she defined as winning the war,
setting the foundations for a lasting peace, and assuring jobs for all
afterward. She constantly asked herself and the people to whom she
spoke, especially after visits to the wounded in the hospitals, How
can it ever be made worthwhile to them?"

A new problem arose with the president's reelection. Some of
her friends urged that she be more selective about the tasks she
undertook. They did so in view of the prodigious respect that she
commanded everywhere and also in view of the president's increased
frailty. Shortly after the election, she had a talk with Franklin and
Harry about the next four years. It so impressed the latter that he
recorded it almost verbatim.

> Mrs. Roosevelt urged the President very strongly to keep
> in the forefront of his mind the domestic situation because
> she felt there was a real danger of his losing American pub-
> lic opinion in his foreign policy if he failed to follow through
> on the domestic implications of his campaign promises. She
> particularly hoped the President would not go to Great
> Britain and France and receive great demonstrations abroad
> for the present, believing that that would not sit too well
> with the American people.

> She impressed on both of us that we must not be satis-
> fied with merely making campaign pledges; the President
> being under moral obligation to see his domestic reforms
> through, particularly the organizing of our domestic life in
> such a way as to give everybody a job. She emphasized that
> this was an overwhelming task and she hoped neither the
> President nor I thought it was settled in any way by making
> speeches.

About this memo Robert Sherwood, Hopkins's biographer, wrote
that the unique function she performed for her husband was "as the
keeper and constant spokesman for her husband's conscience."

She added an element to government that was defined not by
the positions she held but by the spirit with which she infused it. She
had bucked and resisted the limitations imposed on her as Franklin's

wife, but she had also used the opportunities in a way that made her unique among first ladies.

"Maybe I'd do the most useful job if I just became 'a good wife' and waited on F.D.R.," she wrote, in answer to Esther Lape's plea that she cut her schedule down to essentials. But being "a good wife" had its difficulties. Just as her offer to help with the mail had been rebuffed by Franklin before his first inauguration, so he preferred to keep her at arm's length, and never more so than after his reelection, when he seemed withdrawn into himself almost to the point of indifference to his surroundings. Officials like Henry Wallace, James Byrnes, and Frances Perkins had the impression that to cite Eleanor's support of a project or candidate did not improve its chances with him. "[A]t the present time he fights everything she is for," Wallace wrote in his diary.

She professed relief when she did not have to go with the president to Warm Springs at Thanksgiving and then peppered him with

Eleanor and Franklin with thirteen of their grandchildren, January 20, 1945.

critical letters about the rightist cast of his State Department choices after the resignation of Cordell Hull. A few weeks later she was distressed when he found reasons to keep her from accompanying him to Yalta. Her messages and letters to him both at Yalta and Warm Springs had a confident, resolute tone when she inveighed against some of the State Department appointments and urged his intervention on behalf of Wallace's nomination as head of the Reconstruction Finance Corporation as well as secretary of commerce. Her messages were those of a national leader in her own right, precise, relevant, and serious. They may have had the opposite effect than she intended. At Yalta Franklin handed them over to Byrnes, who was with him, with "little indication of personal interest," wrote the former Justice.

She wanted to go to Yalta, but whether her presence would have changed matters is speculative. Later she said she had been shocked when she learned that Estonia, Latvia, and Lithuania "had been left with the Soviet Union," but whether with Stalin's armies on the ground it might have been possible to prevent incorporation is questionable, even if the president had listened to her. The news leak about the agreement to give Soviet Russia three extra votes in the UN General Assembly startled her: "I just don't think FDR would be stupid enough to make secret agreements." Yet if she had been at Yalta, she might have yielded to the same considerations that moved Roosevelt and Churchill.

The president returned to this country to address Congress on the results at Yalta sitting down with the heavy leg braces off. Both at the White House and at Hyde Park, where he went before he left for Warm Springs, she saw the telltale signs that he was wearing out. "He no longer *wants* to drive his own car at Hyde Park—lets her drive which he never did before," an old friend wrote, "and lets her mix cocktails if Colonel Boettiger is not present." But, Eleanor said, after describing the president's plans to revive the Sahara and the Tigris-Euphrates Valley, "*I'm* all ready to sit back. *He's* still looking forward to more work."

A few weeks later she was called out of a meeting and asked to return to the White House, where she learned of his death. Her cable to her sons read: HE DID HIS JOB TO THE END AS HE WOULD WANT YOU TO DO.

TOP: *Mrs. Roosevelt and her children in front of the White House as the president's body arrives at the executive mansion.* BOTTOM: *In the Rose Garden at Hyde Park at the funeral. Anna is at left, Elliott at right.*

Eisenhower and Charles de Gaulle visited FDR's grave in July and August, respectively.

11

BEREFT AND FREE

Eleanor is so candid in her letters in describing her soul's confusions as well as certainties that the onlooker is tempted to make inferences about her hesitations and reticences, and nowhere more so than in her relations with Franklin. She had written Esther Lape, who had urged her to stay more closely by the ailing president, that it was difficult for her to do because there was "no fundamental love" upon which to draw.

Never had events thrust her more to the forefront as Franklin's surrogate than at his death. Never had she performed the role more faultlessly, doing what she thought he would have wished. Slowly her feelings began to change, as she no longer had to defend her own independence by resistance and opposition. Even though she did not acknowledge the change to herself, she repeatedly stressed in the weeks after his death how much she had relied upon him intellectually. She did not say that she did so emotionally, and perhaps it is the sentimentality of her children and friends that led them to say she never let go of anyone she had ever loved. "That is what she told me," Esther Lape asserted about Eleanor's denial of an emotional bond. "That was her story. Maybe she even half believed it. But I didn't. I don't think she ever stopped loving someone she loved."

Among the most poignant passages in the second volume of her autobiography, *This I Remember* (1949), are those that deal with her efforts to serve Franklin in the years after her discovery that there was a side to his nature whose satisfaction by others she had to discipline herself to tolerate. It was a difficult relationship, but they had managed on its basis to work out ways of enormous benefit to mankind. Robert Sherwood called her the "conscience" of the New Deal. Humility as well as a distaste for narrow moral attitudes kept her from acknowledging so pivotal a role in events. Yet twelve years later she admitted in a recorded interview, "In a way, my conscience bothered him. And that's [a] perfectly natural thing. He was a very human person in a great many ways." Whatever their disagreements, she also said in *This I Remember,* "I have never known a man who gave one a sense of greater security."

There were anxieties at the time of his death that she kept private. She had learned of Mrs. Rutherfurd's presence at the White House and at Warm Springs. Anna's failure to tell her shadowed the relationship between mother and daughter for several months and then became a matter of memory rather than feeling. She also was upset by a move of army intelligence to deny a friend a commission, a move that was overruled by Secretary Stimson and General Marshall in deference to her. She did not permit personal worries to intrude on the majesty and solemnity of the events that attended the president's burial and moved through them composed and controlled, a figure of dignity, trying to do things as he might have wished.

"The story is over," she told a newswoman who was waiting on the sidewalk outside her Washington Square apartment house when she returned to New York. The same paradoxical fear that important changes in her life heralded personal dimunition had attended her entry into the White House. It meant her finish as an independent personality, she was sure, as well as farewell to associates, causes, and organizations that had come to regard her as a mainstay. Instead, as historians have written, she had "remade the role of First Lady." Now, with Franklin's death, she again thought she would disappear from sight, her powers and emotions narrowly confined.

The outpouring of love, grief, and fear occasioned by his death all centered on her. President Truman wanted her at his side. Newspapers all over the world asked for her column. She discounted the latter. "Of course it is curiosity as to how I handle this period and will soon wear off." As the world's sense of bereavement welled about her, Hick wrote comfortingly, "You are like that—people instinctively turn to you for comfort, even when you are in trouble yourself."

Eleanor's executive mind already was busy. She saw her job as first of all "disentangling things at Hyde Park and getting appraisals made and the children's choices." She refused to consider the work she might personally do but saw clearly that with Franklin's death a period of history had ended, "and we have to start again under our own momentum and wonder what we can achieve." Things had to be done "for the children's sake and for the sake of FDR's wishes," so she discouraged job offers and laughed away the friends who proposed to constitute themselves as a "brain trust" for her.

But in her column, which she resumed writing a week after Franklin's death, she quietly served notice to the watching world. "Because I was the wife of the President certain restictions were imposed upon me. Now I am on my own and I hope to write as a newspaperwoman." She also made it abundantly clear that she had views on such issues as renewal of the Fair Employment Practices Commission (FEPC) and intended to state them, not only to President Truman, who invited them, but to the country as well. She was not only a custodian of Franklin's ideals but a liberal leader in her own right.

When Moscow, speaking through the French Communists, savaged Earl Browder, the leader of the American Communists, for "revisionism," meaning his cooperative attitude with the government, she read it as a changing attitude by the Soviet government that she felt had better be cleared up in the interests of peace. She further warned that "we will not tolerate" efforts by American Communists to force their ideas on the United States." Though spoken by America's foremost liberal, it is doubtful that this warning had any effect on the Soviet government. She herself wanted to go to Moscow but as a journalist. She consulted President Truman, who advised her it was not timely, so she postponed the trip.

"Whatever Mary [Wollstonecraft] saw served to start her mind upon some theory," wrote Virginia Woolf. So it was with Eleanor as she emerged from the shock of Franklin's death. The explorations that the heart prompted were laced with the realism of experience. Sidney Hillman invited her to head the National Citizens Political Action Committee, of which the CIO was the mainstay. She turned it down because the position carried large responsibilities without commensurate powers and she disliked the influence of the left wing upon the organization. Though she believed a ginger group working on the parties was desirable, her leadership of such a group would only irritate the regular party.

Another firm decision required little debate in her mind. She refused to run for office herself, as Secretary of Interior Ickes proposed. All her boys had political ambitions, and she did not want to be in competition with them—"I want them to feel in the future that any running for public office will be done by them."

The months after Franklin's death were, in fact, chiefly occupied with her children. Family meetings, usually at Hyde Park, were not placid affairs. Her children were all robust individuals, quite vocal, ambitious. The arguments among them over the division of Franklin's estate, the disposal of the Hyde Park land, the books to be written, the movies produced, became vehement. "Money brings out the worst in everyone I think!" she wrote a friend. After one rancorous family meeting, they all turned to her and begged her to be the family arbiter. She concurred but stipulated, "I want you to agree that you will never say anything derogatory about each other or make any other kind of remark that can be so construed, and you will never allow people in your presence to say anything that will reflect on the integrity and character of the family."

Despite her public interests and concern for humanity, she was intensely home- and family-minded. She wanted Hyde Park and her cottage to continue to be "home." She clung to its association with Franklin. She was happy when James retrieved Fala, Franklin's dog, from Margaret Suckley, the distant cousin and Hyde Park neighbor who had been with Franklin at Warm Springs when he died. Fala's presence and Tommy's added to a sense that Hyde Park remained "home" and that she was not wholly alone. Most of all, Elliott's decision to settle there contributed to her feeling of relatedness to place and time. The purchase of the land from the estate that she undertook when Elliott expressed an interest in running it as a farm involved bitter disputes among the children. But in the end she prevailed. She would not continue to live at Hyde Park, she warned the others, unless she was able to buy the land around her cottage. Elliott's decision to live there, she later wrote in the dedication to *This I Remember,* "was also a factor in the completion of this book. Had I not stayed here it would have been far more difficult to write and I might never have done so."

As summer turned into fall her schedule again assumed hectic proportions. In October she was sixty-one. She told one interviewer that she was warning friends that the day would come when she sat by a fire "with a little lace cap on my head and a shawl about my shoulders." Though she nodded her head to the passage of time, such idylls were not seriously meant, and she assured another interviewer that what had been true of Theodore Roosevelt was "true of all Roosevelts. They can always keep busy."

She did not question President Truman's decision to drop the atom bomb in midsummer but quickly lent her support at war's end to the extraordinary effort led by scientists to bring the dread weapon under international control. That involved the United Nations, which she considered her husband's most important legacy to the world. She wanted to be associated with this second effort to bring order to the relations among states. She had been an interested onlooker in Woodrow Wilson's time but wanted a more active part in the second and discreetly suggested Hyde Park as a site for the new world organization.

So when the telephone rang and President Truman asked her to serve as a delegate to the first meeting of the General Assembly in London, although her first reaction was to protest her lack of experience in foreign affairs and her ignorance of parliamentary procedure, she finally concluded she had a duty to accept. Because of her connection with FDR, she told herself, delegates would be reminded of his high hopes for the organization. Truman's selection of her as one of the United States delegates was a tribute to her husband, she said; she attributed to him the creation of opportunities for her to be of use. But she herself would bring to the first meeting some special qualities that she also thought worth mentioning—the desire to understand other nations' problems, good will toward their peoples, and a belief that cooperation in this great new enterprise would be eased by personal trust and friendship.

Just before New Year's Day 1946, together with other members of the United States delegation, she boarded the liner *Queen Elizabeth*, which was still a troopship, for the passage across the Atlantic. The United Nations might not be "final and perfect," she told reporters, but if the atom bomb did nothing more, "it scared people to the point" of doing "something about preventing war or there is a chance that there might be a morning when we would not wake up."

She also said—and perhaps it reflects her feelings about the way she lived the White House years—"very impersonally . . . I was lost somewhere deep down inside myself. That is the way I felt and worked until I left the White House." Now on shipboard, she exclaimed, "For the first time in my life I can say just what I want. For your information it is wonderful to feel free."

Did she put that comment off the record because she did not even want to hint that all through the White House years she had been "a stranger" to Franklin, as she once had put it? Or because she realized the country was not ready yet for an independent woman?

TOP: *The United States delegation departing in 1945 on the* Queen Elizabeth *for the first General Assembly of the United Nations. From left, Senator Tom Connally (D.-Tex.), Senator Arthur H. Vandenberg (R.-Mich.), Edward R. Stettinius, Jr., U. S. Representative on the Security Council, and Mrs. Roosevelt.* LEFT: *Mrs. Roosevelt makes an observation to Secretary of State George C. Marshall at the 1947 General Assembly. In the background is Francis B. Sayre, an alternate member of the U. S. delegation.*

To President Truman she was the "First Lady of the World."

Or was it that flawless sense of tact that kept her from saying anything ungracious about life with her late husband?

There came a hushed moment at the opening in ravaged London when heads turned and bowed toward Eleanor Roosevelt, still garbed in black, as the president of the General Assembly, Paul Henri-Spaak, invoked with reverential care the memory of her husband:

> Among them there is one delegate to whom I wish to extend particularly sympathy and tribute. I refer to her who bears the most illustrious and respected of all names. I do not think it would be possible to begin at this Assembly without mentioning her and the name of the late President Roosevelt and expressing our conviction that his disappearance was a great grief to us all and an irreparable loss.

Until her death seventeen years later it would always be thus—she remained Franklin's surrogate, the living reminder of a departed leader and his hopes for his nation and the world; at the same time she was a figure in her own right, conscious of a vocation of leadership and what was required of it. Winston Churchill perceived the double meaning of her presence. It was six years later. She had come

In April 1948 Mrs. Roosevelt went to England for the unveiling of Britain's memorial statue to FDR. At the ceremony in Grosvenor Square are, from left, Major Hooker, Queen Elizabeth, the Queen Mother Mary, Mrs. Roosevelt, Prime Minister Clement Attlee, King George, and Viscount Greenwood, chairman of the Memorial Committee.

to London for the unveiling of the country's statue of FDR in Grosvenor Square. Later that day at a Pilgrim's dinner Churchill, who was on the eve of returning to office, spoke:

> Many of us know what we owe to our wives in life's varied journeys. Mrs. Roosevelt has made her own distinctive and personal contribution to the generous thought of modern society. . . . [W]e must ascribe to Mrs. Roosevelt the marvellous fact that a crippled man, the victim of a cruel affliction was able for more than ten years to ride the storms of peace and war. The debt that we owe to President Roosevelt is also owed to her. I am sure that she feels round her tonight, in this old parent land and in this great company, the esteem and affection of the whole British people.

At the United Nations with Marion Anderson. One of the pivotal events in the black liberation struggle had been Anderson's concert at the Lincoln Memorial after the Daughters of the American Revolution had denied her the use of Constitution Hall. Eleanor's resignation as a result of that denial had "focused worldwide attention on the episode," said Negro leader Walter White.

Churchill's graceful tribute must be qualified. A man of his time, he accepted unquestioningly man's role as ruler and woman's as helpmeet. But Eleanor Roosevelt was ahead of her time. She was an

independent personality prepared to pay the price of feminine self-reliance and egalitarianism in loneliness and sacrifice.

She was considered, as President Truman stated it, "the First Lady of the World." She earned the title largely as the result of her work at the United Nations as "the hardest working delegate." By the time the United States delegation left shipboard in January 1946, she had mastered the heaps of documents that were daily delivered to her stateroom, attended all delegation meetings, received briefings from many of "the bright young men" on the State Department staff, sat in often with reporters when they interviewed officials, feeling, she said, in a characteristic gesture of self-depreciation, as if she had been to school and was "getting a disciplined mind again." Her ever-present sense of duty and the realization that a woman had to try harder did not permit her to loaf, but she mischievously noted that some of he men did, and their vanities amused her. "I'm so glad I never *feel* important, it does complicate life." The men on the delegation, especially the Republicans John Foster Dulles and Senator Arthur Vandenberg, approved her assignment to the Assembly's Economic and Social Committee [Committee Three] as they considered it "a safe spot." The men, she noted, were accustomed to relegating women in public life to roles they considered without political hazard. Such preconceptions changed as the session advanced. Even she acknowledged to her daughter, "The old lady holds up very well under the load of work here & believe me it is formidable."

The State Department quickly realized that in her it had a priceless asset, not only as the "willing workhorse," as a relative had described her role as a volunteer in World War I, but as a symbol of America's and the world's hopes in the UN. She was the main speaker at the Albert Hall meeting to welcome the delegates to the General Assembly. Privately she lamented that there were "too many elderly public men" about "who cling to their jobs. Too many gray hairs like my own on the floor." Her words at Albert Hall, however, showed the way to action at the UN despite the controversies over the war's spoils that had emerged among the victors. "We must be willing to learn the lesson that cooperation may imply compromise but if it brings a world advance it is a gain for each individual nation."

Her natural demeanor, which combined majesty with modesty, was irresistible. Her presence made an occasion, whether it was luncheon at Buckingham Palace or a party in the rooms of the Byelo-Russian delegation. At the end of the days' sessions she contentedly joined young associates to eat at the embassy canteen and with the same unaffected thoughtfulness turned over hard-to-come-by eggs sent to her by some grateful English friends to Representative Sol Bloom, a fellow member of the United States delegation. She addressed the Pilgrims, the only woman to do so in the many years of that illustrious society's dedication to Anglo-American friendship, and she spoke reassuringly to a large group of English brides of American GIs who were about to journey to an unknown land.

All this activity was fueled by clear and urgent ideas of what the United Nations should be. There were some, especially after the dropping of the atom bomb, who urged revision of the UN Charter in the direction of world federalism or world government, including the ending of the power to veto UN action. She was an old hand at not permitting the best to be the enemy of the good. That had been the history of many of the legislative battles associated with the New Deal. "I wish everyone would make this work first," she now replied to the world federalist appeals. Nations had to learn to "crawl together," before they were ready to "run together. . . . Why our own Congress wouldn't stand for doing away with the veto power and Russia is back in Daniel Boone's days so why should she?" The "biggest job" for UN statesmen was to make people at home feel that "this is their machinery which they must use to build peace, but they will have to keep it oiled and make it run."

Her own temperament as well as years at Franklin's side had given her a clear conception of what it was to lead. "They are rude and arrogant," she said of Dulles and Vandenberg. "Jimmy Byrnes's overcordiality isn't right either." In general she distrusted the politician in the role of statesman. "I am interested in the way all the legislators [on the delegation] react. I think not having strong convictions they doubt their ability to defend a position which they take so they cannot decide on any position and go on arguing pros and cons endlessly."

Her doubts about the politicians on the delegation matched very definite views about United States relations with the Soviet Union and Great Britain. She doubted the United States and Great Britain "must line up to keep the Russians in hand. I think we must be fair and stand for what we believe is right and let them, either or both, side with us. We have had that leadership and must recapture it." Her seat in the Assembly hall at the end of the delegation placed her closest to the Soviet delegation. She tried to make personal friends of them. Andrei Vishinsky, Stalin's prosecutor in the Moscow trials, led the Soviet delegation. "He looks like a middle western banker," she exclaimed mischievously. She sought out Andrei Gromyko, a much younger man, who was also the Soviet ambassador to the United

States. She talked at length with this gray and frosty Assembly neighbor and hoped he considered her a "friend." But in general she found the Russians "very rarely smile. They come to every session and stay through the end." They were "hard to work with because everything has to be decided in Moscow."

The Assembly's corridors provided a chance for the off-the-record exchanges with other diplomats that are the preliminaries to more formal agreements. It was a form of civilized contact that she enjoyed and at which she excelled. She sensed Soviet rawness and insecurity and made it a point to be agreeable. By the end of the first Assembly, she had a crisp, four-point program for dealing with them: Have convictions; Be friendly; Stick to your beliefs as they do to theirs; Work as hard as they do.

"Chance does nothing that has not been prepared beforehand," says de Toqueville. As tension and conflict superseded wartime unity, the issue that most dramatically signaled the rupture came to a head in her committee. It was dealing with the issue of what was to be done with the more than a million refugees in displaced persons camps. The Soviet Union and its allies insisted on forced repatriation. Many of the refugees were opponents of the communist regimes that were seizing power in their countries. They rightly feared repatriation meant death. The communist world saw the DP camps as centers of "revanchism" and future threats to their stability, while the right of political asylum was axiomatic in Western thinking. Mrs. Roosevelt and Andrei Vishinsky emerged as the spokesmen for the two approaches, including the Soviet demand that the United Nations bar "propaganda" from the camps. The men on the U.S. delegation were grateful to her for taking on the commissar. Her essential thesis was that it took "years of stability" to recognize there were "human rights for those who think in a way you think wrong," but such rights were indispensable. "We defeated the Russians on the three points we disagreed on, they were all fundamental, and I'm afraid while I was brief I was clear in my opposition."

She still sought to keep personal relations with her Russian adversaries on an even keel and noted that Vishinsky was "cordiality itself" and that when they said goodbye he remarked, "Madame, when are you coming to Russia?"

Only fourteen women were among the delegates, alternates, and advisors to the first Assembly. At her call, all had crowded in to her sitting room at Claridge's. The group called on the secretariat and the member governments to use more women and to face up to women's issues. It also called on women to equip themselves for such

133

work and "to come forward." She hoped for more women in the UN in the future. "They participated so fully in fighting the war," her column pointed out; moreover, the United Nations Charter stipulated "complete equality" between the sexes. But she kept the more outspoken advocates of feminism at arm's length. "I am still opposed to an equal rights amendment," she wrote in June.

> We cannot change the fact that women are different from men. It's true that some women can do more than men and some can do men's jobs better than men can do them. But the fact that they are different cannot be changed, and it is fortunate for us that this is the case. The best results are always obtained when men and women work together, with the recognition that their abilities and contributions may differ but that, in every field, they supplement each other.

A final assignment at the Assembly resulted from the United States Army's request that she fly to Germany and spend a day at Zeilsheim, where Jewish survivors of the concentration camps had built a monument to the six million Jewish dead. "I answered from an aching heart. When will our consciences grow so tender that we will act to prevent human misery rather than avenge it?" The next day in an almost completely destroyed Berlin, when German newsmen asked whether the whole German nation was responsible for the war, "I answered what to me seems obvious. All the people of Germany have to accept responsibility for having trusted a leadership which first brought such misery to groups of people within their own nation and later created world chaos." As army officials escorted her through the ruins of the great hall that led to Hitler's office, she thought of "the utter smallness of a human being who needed so much outward grandeur to build up his own sense of importance."

At the Assembly's end, Dulles said to her, "I feel I must tell you that when you were appointed I thought it terrible and now I think your work has been fine."

"So—against odds," she wrote home, "the women inch forward."

12

UNWILLING COLD WARRIOR

ELEANOR HAD LOOKED FORWARD to peacetime not only as an end to hazard and destruction but as a new start for mankind and the better regulation of its affairs. The first session of the General Assembly in London had shown instead that victory ushered in disunity among the Big Three. Each of the great powers scrambled for the spoils, guided by its own interests, history, and values. Amid such turbulent events she remained poised and calm, pressing steadily for her husband's vision as embodied in the United Nations Charter.

Like her husband, she valued getting along with people. At home she had been accustomed to the maintenance of good personal relations with political opponents. The latter usually had included the Oyster Bay Roosevelts, led by her redoubtable cousin Alice Longworth. Stung by Alice's attacks, Franklin had wanted to exclude her from White House parties. Eleanor had demurred and prevailed. Civility and good manners in political disputes seemed as natural to her as breathing. She did not consider talking with opponents trading with the enemy.

Nevertheless, she was a woman of principle who lived democracy. Despite a determination to get along with the Russians, she found herself compelled by her nature to oppose them. Five years later Claire Booth Luce, a long-time political foe, would say of her not only that she was "the best-loved woman in the world" but that it was "safe to say that her resistance to Soviet Communism is a more potent factor in winning the cold war than an extra billion dollars of Marshall Plan aid."

She had not wanted matters to go that way. A trip to Russia remained as high on her agenda at the end of the London Assembly as it had been in 1945 when Edward J. Flynn, one of her husband's closest political associates, who went to Moscow after Yalta, brought back word that the Russians wanted to see her. Harry Hopkins after his talks with Stalin in May 1945 at President Truman's request also had urged her to go. The last letter she received from him not long before she boarded the *Queen Elizabeth* for the General Assembly lamented the downard course of United States-Soviet relations: "I think we are doing almost everything we can to break with Russia which seems so unnecessary to me." In the growing dispute between Henry Wallace and President Truman over the latter's "get tough" policy toward Russia and the increasing military emphasis in American policy, she was sympathetic to the secretary and said many of the same things.

She was more than ready to get along with the Russians and was one of the few members of the United States delegation in London who sensed how much Soviet behavior was influenced by insecurity and inexperience. When she spoke of Russia being back in "Daniel Boone days," she meant that Americans especially should be able to appreciate a frontier mentality of distrust and fear of foreigners.

We should think back to the early days of the Republic, when a great many people of the world disapproved of the experiment we were trying. We were suspicious of them and we were antagonistic. We had a chip on our shoulders then, but we are very different now. Our standards have changed, but we must realize that these things take time.

She did not mean that the United States should be weak in its dealings with the Soviets. "We must stand up for our meaning [of democracy]. We must show the Russians we cannot be worn down or tired out." The development of mutual confidence and a willingness to respect the UN charter would take time, she preached tirelessly.

My own approach to any difficulties that emerge among the United Nations is that there is one paramount thing to remember—namely that we have discovered super weapons of destruction. If we wish we can destroy ourselves and our entire civilization. If we do not wish to do this, then we must learn to get on together without war. That entails the success of the UNO.

So when Churchill in March 1946 made his speech at Fulton, Missouri, and in the presence of President Truman spoke of the Iron Curtain that Russia had lowered across Europe and urged an Anglo-American alliance based on the West's monopoly of the atom bomb and less reliance on the United Nations, she used her column to answer. She was against any division of the world "into armed camps. . . . [T]he old way of counting on our own individual force seems still to have a strong hold on us. . . . We still question whether our different political and economic systems can exist side by side in the world. . . . We still loathe to give up the old power and attempt to build a new kind of power and security in the world. I am convinced that this timidity is perhaps the greatest danger in the world today."

She and Churchill were old hands at political controversy, and neither allowed their disagreements at this time to impair the solemnity of Churchill's visit to Hyde Park to place a wreath on FDR's grave.

She remained at the UN until the end of Truman's second term. Throughout her service there she pressed the United States to use the United Nations, to make it in deeds as well as words the cornerstone of its foreign policy. But the eruption of Soviet-American tension, a reality that she faced in her work at the world organization, compelled Washington to redirect its policy. It placed greater emphasis on military power. It set about building a Western alliance. She went along unwillingly. Her hope continued to be the United Nations.

Her Washington days had taught her that in a democracy strength emanates from the grass roots. The place to work, she had advised organizations that gravitated toward Washington, was in the congressional districts. The United Nations, she now said, was only strong as its members allowed it to be, and that in turn depended on the peoples in the member states.

> The job of writing a peace and then building a peaceful world through the United Nations Organization based on that peace is not the job alone of the government officials. . . . It is the job of the peoples of the world, and it will be done only if they put their strength back of their representatives and insist that the main objectives of keeping peace in the world shall always be in the forefront of everybody's mind.

It never seemed to her that the issue was "if" the UN succeeds. It

Eleanor addresses a plenary session of the General Assembly, October 20, 1949.
Carlos Romulo of the Philippines is in the president's chair.

Accompanying Winston Churchill in 1946 to the Rose Garden at Hyde Park, where his companion-at-arms lay buried.

At a 1949 testimonial dinner for Walter Reuther—"a rather intelligent young labor leader," she had called him in 1944, urging financier Bernard Baruch to meet with him.

was the "alternative to chaos, therefore I've never allowed myself to be pessimistic."

Yet whatever her criticisms of her own government's policies, she was unable to ignore the crudities of Soviet behavior as it confronted her at the UN. The origins of the Cold War, whether signaled by Churchill's Iron Curtain speech or Stalin's address the month before to Moscow electors, have been endlessly analyzed by scholars. Was it triggered by the United States or the Soviet Union? Was it a protective response to domestic disintegrative forces, or expansionist and acquisitive? How much a role did personalities play, especially the paranoid personality of Russia's absolutist ruler, Stalin? Was it powered by history, ideology, or geopolitics, or perhaps an admixture of all of them? The questions are endless. The answers in the absence of Soviet and East European archives are self-serving, or at any rate ambiguous.

In the spring of 1946 she had her second run-in with Soviet

truculence. A preparatory human rights commission had been established to draft an international bill of rights. Her appointment to it and election as chairman was by acclamation. The permanent Soviet delegate arrived belatedly to its sessions and blandly asked that his predecessor's concurrences with the decisions that had been taken be stricken from the record. She refused. "No amount of argument ever changes what your Russian delegate says or how he votes," she wrote afterwards. "It is the most exasperating thing in the world. . . . If I have patience enough, in a year from now perhaps the Russians may come with a different attitude."

She was patient but a few weeks later she dropped plans to visit the USSR. "Just say I am going to be at Hyde Park working on my autobiography," she told the *Herald-Tribune*. Earlier she had written her son Jimmy the real reason. "The heat and tension over Iran I fear would make it hard for them to trust me and let me write freely and see things." Her face-to-face experience with the Russians at the UN made her cautious about endorsing Elliott's interpretations of FDR's wartime disagreements with Churchill in his book *As He Saw It,* which she had encouraged Elliott to write. She had heard Franklin say many of the things Elliott reported. She very carefully held back, however, from endorsing his conclusion that British colonialism and American militarism were to blame for the disruption of Big Three unity. "We must get together with Russia," she wrote in her column, "but it must be a two-way matter."

Later events that year strengthened a growing feeling that Russia was basically responsible for the Cold War that had begun to rage. At the end of August 1946 Tito's Yugoslavs had shot down two unarmed American transport planes that had wandered over the Yugoslav border. In the ensuing uproar, the Soviet Union backed up the Yugoslavs. The latter's belligerence angered her. "It seems, too, a trifle ironic to have American planes shot down, and Americans possibly killed, by planes and ammunition which had probably been acquired through lend-lease from this country." It was an "unwarranted and cruel attack" and affected her feeling about getting along with Russia. "I have always wanted cooperation with Russia," she wrote. "We have an obligation to meet other nations halfway in friendliness and understanding, but they have that obligation, too—and these latest developments show no realization of their responsibility." The events that attended Henry Wallace's resignation from Truman's cabinet also jolted her hope of getting on with Russia. She was troubled that Wallace had many communist-minded people in his entourage. Nor did she like his concept of a world divided into spheres of influence. Wallace had been booed by the Communists in his audience at Madison Square Garden. They did not like the sections of his speech that dealt with Russian obligations and rights. "Why an American audience should boo Mr. Wallace for saying what he did about Russia and the need for Russia to come halfway in her contacts with us, is beyond my understanding."

The issue of international control of atomic energy crystallized her dislike of Soviet attitudes in the UN as well as her uneasiness about where Wallace was heading. She had supported Truman's decision to drop the atom bomb and thus speed the end of the war with Japan. But she understood immediately that the unleashing of the atom's awesome power for good or evil made the success of the United Nations imperative.

International control of atomic energy was the alternative, she believed, to the armaments race and, ultimately, war. She enthusiastically supported the Baruch Plan, which originally was drafted by Dean Acheson and David Lilienthal of the TVA. Under its provisions, knowledge and control over atomic energy would be turned over to the UN in stages. She regarded it as generous and realistic. Wallace criticized it, especially its "stage-by-stage" feature. "We are telling the Russians that if they are 'good boys' we may eventually turn over our knowledge of atomic energy to them," he said. Baruch was a good friend of Mrs. Roosevelt's and, believing that Wallace had misstated his position, asked her to ask Wallace to meet him. She promptly sent Wallace a telegram to that effect. "Where was I wrong?" Wallace asked when they met. The pertinent parts of the record were read to him, according to Baruch. "Slowly Wallace agreed that the idea of in 'stages' was sound," Baruch told his biographer. Wallace proposed to Baruch that they work out a new plan to show they were in agreement, but then, according to Baruch, he "reneged."

The episode shook her confidence in Wallace's judgment. It weakened her sympathy for his general position, although she had thought his letter at the time of his resignation voicing his misgivings about United States policy, "a good letter" and "a fair analysis of the reasons for international tension." She agreed with Wallace that "the test of any situation is to put yourself in the other man's place—and we have not done that very successfully in our attitude toward Russia." She added, "the basic thing to be held in mind is that we want peace and that it cannot exist if the United States and Russia do not find a way to live together in the world."

She stuck to this basic conviction even though at the end of the year Soviet Foreign Minister V. M. Molotov in the UN "impugned our motives in our plan for atomic control and development and attacked Bernard Baruch personally." Molotov's vituperative speech was a prelude to Soviet refusal to accept the United States plan. By the end of 1946 the plan was dead and the most gigantic arms race in mankind's history was under way.

Wallace's attack on the Baruch Plan contributed to Mrs. Roosevelt's readiness to help found Americans for Democratic Action, a liberal organization that excluded Communists from positions of leadership. She favored the unity of American liberals, "and if the Progressive Citizens of America [PCA; the Wallace organization] could remove from its leadership the communist element, I do not see any reason why ADA and PCA should not work together." 'Her support of the ADA neutralized the efforts of Wallace and the PCA to portray themselves as the true heirs of Roosevelt.

Amid the fissurings and breakup of Big Three unity, she never abandoned the view that there was no alternative to peace and that the best hope for it was through the United Nations. She found it reassuring when President Truman replaced Secretary of State Byrnes, a politician whom she did not trust, with General George C. Marshall, a man in whose integrity she had complete confidence. Nevertheless, Truman's proposal to aid Greece and Turkey with arms and other military aid and to do it outside of the UN upset her. She did not disagree with the administration's overall policy of the "containment" of communism but urged that it be done through economic reconstruction and under the aegis of the United Nations. "I naturally grieve to see this country do anything which harms the UN. If we could have given help for relief and rehabilitation on a purely non-political basis, and then have insisted that the UN join us on any political or policy basis . . . I would have felt far happier than I do now. . . ."

Her opposition to the unilateralist implications of the Truman Doctrine was not eased by the State Department emissary who was dispatched to explain the new policy to her. "I hope that never again this type of action will be taken without at least consulting with the Secretary General and with our permanent member on the Security Council beforehand." She admonished Acting Secretary of State Dean Acheson along these lines and informed Senator Vandenberg, the Republican spokesman on foreign policy, who felt, as she did, that the UN should not be ignored, "I still feel that our attitude toward Russia should be less negative and more a comprehensive plan for the revival of the world, since it always seems to be that a positive program has more strength than a negative one."

In her lengthy correspondence with President Truman, she deprecated the Truman Doctrine as little more than a "taking over [of] Mr. Churchill's policies in the Near East." It was not the way "to really create a barrier to communism or promote democracy." When General Marshall in April 1947 returned from another fruitless session of the Council of Foreign Ministers, she asked anxiously in her column: "Has he come to a conclusion as to what a comprehensive plan for world recovery must contain or is he still groping?" But then she supported Marshall in his historic offer when a few weeks later at Harvard the general voiced American readiness to aid a European-drafted plan for the restoration of its economic health. She hailed it as "very constructive." Communist exploitation of a shattered Europe was a fact, and General Marshall's offer to help it to its feet seemed to her the way to stop it.

Again, as with Russia's opposition to the Baruch plan, that country's refusal to cooperate strengthened an awareness that whatever the shortcomings of United States policy, Soviet Russia carried the chief responsibility for the emerging division of Europe. She concluded it was deliberate Soviet policy to make matters as disagreeable as possible for the United States in Europe in the hope the United States might wash its hands of the continent and leave Moscow the dominant force there. And as if to dramatize Soviet Russia's policy of "the worse the better" in Europe, Molotov walked out of the Paris conference convened to launch the Marshall Plan. Though she was unhappy about the plan's independence from the UN and urged the invitation of the secretary-general to its founding meetings, she did not press the issue with General Marshall.

She was always ready to look at matters through the other fellow's eyes, but she found it impossible to see Soviet policy as a defensive measure. Communist purges and seizures of power were silencing all independent political voices there and culminated in early 1946 in the overthrow of Czech democracy and the death, either by suicide or defenestration, of a familiar figure in the West, Jan Masaryk, Czechoslovakia's foreign minister. That event brought home to many doubters "the grim face" of brute Soviet power and totalitarianism.

The West reacted to Soviet aggression by merging the areas of occupation in West Germany into a single economic unit, a preliminary to the creation of a West German state. The USSR countered with a blockade of West Berlin. It hoped to force a Western withdrawal from Berlin and then Germany. Events seemed to be moving toward war. "I do not think I have been as alarmed before," she wrote Truman, "but I have become very worried and since we always

144

have to sit down together when war comes to an end, I think before we have a Third World War, we should sit down together." She begged Marshall to consider a peace mission of "a picked group" that would meet with the representatives of Great Britain and Soviet Russia "around a table before we actually get to a point where we are in a war."

Both Truman and Marshall sought to reassure her. The hope of peace, they said, rested in the European Recovery Program backed by the United States military build-up. "Anyone can see," she agreed, "that we cannot sit quiet in this situation and also that mere words get us nowhere at this time." Her proposal for a peace mission to Stalin was discussed but set aside only to surface during the 1948 election when Truman announced he was sending Chief Justice Fred M. Vinson to Moscow. The mission was dropped when General Marshall in Paris for the 1948 General Assembly opposed it and it was widely criticized as a campaign gesture.

The 1948 General Assembly took place during the height of the Berlin blockade. "The Russians attack verbally in every committee," she wrote. "Russia's attitude is discouraging and Marshall I think believes it is a case of outstaying and outbluffing your adversary but the stake of war is such a high one that this game cannot be played lightheartedly." She still was ready to meet the Russians halfway but was resigned to Soviet inflexibility. ". . . I think it will take a long time to get real understanding with the USSR government. It will be the result of long and patient work. Their government and its representatives think differently. They will have to reach a higher standard of living and not be afraid to let others in and their own out before we can hope for a change."

Her belief in the United Nations did not falter, but she began to question whether bending over backwards with the Russians was effective. She "never again" would compromise "even on words," she told the *Herald-Tribune.* "The Soviets look on this as evidence of weakness rather than as a gesture of good will." In September 1949 President Truman announced that the USSR had successfully tested an atom bomb. She doubted Moscow had a stockpile of bombs, she reassured friends, but added, and it was a measure of how strongly this woman of charity and compassion had come to suspect Soviet purposes, that it would be well to be more on the alert than ever in order to avoid another Pearl Harbor.

13

WHERE DO HUMAN RIGHTS BEGIN?

When will our consciences grow so tender that we will act to prevent human misery rather than avenge it?
—ELEANOR ROOSEVELT

Mrs. Roosevelt wrote James Hendrick, her chief advisor on Human Rights matters, in May 1947: "My husband's estate has not yet been settled. Some of the provisions of his will are interpreted by the trustees in such manner as makes it necessary for me to buy what land I want at Hyde Park from the estate. . . ." She explained that it might be difficult for her to go abroad in August.

> While I deeply regret having to bring personal matters into a public service situation, I feel I owe it to my children to get these matters settled as soon as it is practicable to do so.
>
> I want the Department to feel entirely free to name another person, if I am not able to go to Geneva, to take my place, or if the Department finds it more satisfactory, I shall be glad to resign so a permanent person can be named in my place.

She was then Chairman of the Human Rights Commission, which was halfway finished with its draft of an international bill of rights, an achievement that permanently established her as a world figure. Her willingness to yield this central spot showed how duties and

TOP: *She called the Universal Declaration of Human Rights a "magna carta for mankind."* RIGHT: *"My soul stood erect," Helen Keller wrote to her after the Declaration was approved by the United Nations Assembly.*

responsibilities arranged themselves in her mind after Franklin's death. Success in private functioning always seemed to her more important than the public things she did.

"Home" was her cottage two miles east of the big house and library. She became a familiar figure in the rose garden where Franklin was buried, a tall woman with Fala on a leash who swept into view to greet some dignitary—Churchill, De Gaulle, Khrushchev—who had come to Hyde Park to pay his respects to the dead leader. The rambling structure held many rooms, which she filled with friends, relatives, and associates with whom came conversation, laughter, and love.

She set the pace in the conversational exchanges, rarely allowing them to flag, but sometimes in family conclaves the children gave her the feeling she was the source of their difficulties. Then she sank into a depression that was deep-seated, almost suicidal, but that she kept hidden from all but a few.

During a brief period of 1946 she found herself in a tight financial situation. She estimated her total income based on personal earnings as well as what came from her own securities and Franklin's estate at $80,000. Of that total, $54,000 went for federal and state taxes. That left her—Harry Hooker, her lawyer and old friend, pointed out—$26,000 for living expenses, charities, and pension. He cautioned her not to incur additional expenses. But her earning power turned out to be greater than she expected, especially from her writings and lecturing. These included "My Day," a monthly magazine page, *This I Remember,* the second volume of her autobiography, and her radio and television appearances. She received a $12,000 stipend as a member of the permanent United States Mission at the United Nations but refused the lifetime $5,000 pension that Congress granted her as the widow of a president. By 1947 she no longer had a fear of living beyond her means. In addition she helped the children, contributed to the farm's expenses, and continued to make many, although smaller, contributions. All in all, she lived comfortably.

In August 1946, as she drove herself to New York from Hyde Park, she became drowsy and collided head-on with another car. "I was terrified to think that someone else might have been hurt," she wrote in her column. No one was seriously injured, but she was at fault, as she had immediately announced in her column, to the consternation of her lawyers. For a few months she was without a driver's license and when she regained it drove only in the vicinity of Hyde Park. Her two front teeth had broken off. "Now I shall have

With David Gurewitsch. "I've really taken you into my heart . . ."

two lovely porcelain ones, which will look far better than the rather protruding large teeth which most of the Roosevelts have."

She continued to shape her life in the ways that she wanted it to go. Its most unexpected turn was the maturing of an acquaintance-ship with Dr. David Gurewitsch into love. She was sixty-three, at the end of her middle years, and her ability to love was an unexpected blessing. "Don't ever worry about being a nuisance," she wrote him from Geneva, where the Human Rights Commission was meeting: "I've always liked you and was drawn to you since we first met and the trip (on the plane to Europe) just made me sure that we could be friends. . . . I've really taken you to my heart however, so there need never be a question of bother again. . . . being with you is a joy."

When David protested his shyness, she answered it must be her "old shyness and insecurity" and sought to clarify the relationship of the private and public in her life.

The people I love mean more to me than all the public things even if you do think that public affairs should be my

chief vocation. I only do the public things because there are
a few close people whom I love dearly and who matter to
me above everything else. There are not so many of them
and you are now one of them and I shall just have to try
not to bother you too much!

The relationship with David, who was eighteen years younger,
had its quota of joys and sadness. Its closeness ws the more remarkable because physical passion did not undergird it and each considered the other person unattainable. It seemed to be a condition
of her most ardent friendships that they were unrequited in a physical sense. Shortly after the war she was named as corespondent in a
suit for divorce filed by the wife of Earl Miller, the handsome state
trooper who had been Franklin's bodyguard when he was governor
of New York and who had served as her escort as she had traveled
about the state. They had become lifelong friends. His reply to quer-
ies about the closeness of their relationship was a return query, or
was it a feint? "How do you sleep with someone you call 'Mrs. Roosevelt?' " Her letters to him, as to several others—Nancy Cook, Lorena Hickok, David—were those of a lover.

The recipe for the anguish caused by the knowledge that she
no longer was first in her husband's life, and for the unattainable
loves that followed that discovery, was work. She had learned to
channel her longings into service. She had learned during her White
House years—and it was equally true of the postwar years, when she
emerged as a world leader—that having people close to her kept her
from being swallowed up by public duties. She was part of that small
minority, noted by Freud, who find happiness along the path of love,
and of an even smaller minority who renounce instinctual satisfaction in their pursuit of benevolent love.

That was the private life that was the backdrop to the public.
Eleanor's encounter with Vishinsky over the issue of forced repatriation, her notable espousal at home of the rights of minorities, especially blacks, her identification in the public mind as a figure of
compassion, made her the logical choice by the UN secretary-general, acceded to by President Truman, to lead the task of drafting
an international bill of rights. This had been assigned to the permanent UN organization by its founding conference in San Francisco in 1945. She willingly took on the job. She would show that in
the touchiest of areas, individual rights, the United Nations was
workable. Deeds were the best test of good intentions and high hopes.
She was the chief opponent of the realists in the United States gov-

ernment who sought to downgrade the UN, although all professed commitment to it. A bill that spelled out the universal rights reflecting the common humanity that made "one world" possible would be the best answer to the skeptics.

Beginning with the 1946 meeting of a core group of the Human Rights Commission in the Bronx Annex of Hunter College, she moved in and out of UN halls, a tall, black-garbed figure who carried a black, heavy briefcase, queued up with Secretariat workers in the cafeteria, and elicited from colleagues awed comment about her working habits. The full eighteen-nation commission under her leadership alternated its sessions between Lake Success and Geneva in pursuit of what she hoped might be a "magna carta for mankind."

It worked with drafts of rights prepared by Dr. John Humphrey, the UN's director of its Human Rights Division, and Dr. René Cassin, the distinguished French jurist. Calmly, as if she were handling another unruly brood of children, she presided over the clash of systems in which savants and jurists cited Thomas Aquinas, Confucius, Karl Marx, and the founding fathers. If her "learned colleagues" made statements intelligible to her, she told the members of the drafting committee, they stood a good chance of being understood by people generally. That had often been her function with the president, she added. She professed being "frightened" at being chairman, "since I am not very good at parliamentary law," but she drove the commission hard and was, she said of herself, "almost a slave-driver." It was a two-front struggle. She was, after all, the representative of the president, and considered herself a good soldier, but when she disagreed with the instructions she received, she went back to the State Department and the White House to argue her point. She quickly sensed that the countries the United States was dealing with had their own traditions and interests and that it would be fatal if the United States took the position that it knew everything. The department's preference was to confine the evolving bill to civil and political rights. The Russians, on the other hand, stressed economic and social. "You can't talk civil rights to people who are hungry," she advised Truman and Marshall, and told all and sundry, "we're not living in an American world." The United States position on human rights was changed to accommodate her views.

In the commission itself there were other problems. The delegate of India, a woman, protested the draft's phrase "all men are created equal," because it might be interpreted to leave out women. American women had never felt cut out because the Declaration of

Independence said "all men," Eleanor commented, but yielded when they told her, "if it says 'all men' when we get home it will be all men."

Her most difficult problem was with the Soviet bloc representatives, who came armed with statistics to question United States practices with regard to full employment, housing, and health. She quietly offered to have Soviet experts make on-the-spot appraisals of their claims, if American observers could do the same in the Soviet Union. The offer was not accepted. "Never have I see naivete and cunning so gracefully blended," a State Department observer said admiringly. She was "awfully good" with the Russians, one of her advisors recalled, having "a wonderful capacity for playing it cool." She still had not given up hope of a change in Soviet policy. At the end of the 1947 session of the commission in Geneva, its progress buoyed her. Even the Soviet bloc had abstained rather than voted no, she noted. ". . . [I]t seems perhaps too little to boast about when the Big Four haven't been able to come to any agreement. . . . nevertheless, each small achievement is something to be heralded. . . ."

"I am not a lawyer and four have to sit behind to guide me and they all see different pitfalls in every phrase and I am sometimes in a complete daze!" she lamented. Nevertheless, she continued putting pressure on the commission. If it wanted shorter sessions, its members would have to make shorter speeches. No one should ever tell her that women talk at longer length than men, she commented. She pushed herself equally hard. The lawyers who advised her crowded daily into the mission's car that drove them out to Lake Success and briefed her on the way out. She was quick to pick up what was being suggested, they later testified.

The draft declaration was completed in time for the 1948 General Assembly. No vote was cast against it, the Soviet bloc abstaining. Eighteen months earlier, her chief State Department advisor on human rights after the initial session wrote her, "I get more and more the sensation of something happening in the world which has a chance to override all obstacles, and more and more that this 'something' could never have come into being without you."

The members of the commission and the State Department shared that view. At the Paris General Assembly in 1948, the Communists were on the offensive throughout Europe. She spoke at the Sorbonne in France on "The Struggle for the Rights of Man" and drew the basic issue that separated the communist world and the West. Truman and Marshall had asked her to do so—"to go after

153

the U.S.S.R.," she wrote, "not, thank heavens, claiming perfection but saying that under our system we are achieving these rights and succeeding better than most."

After eighty-five meetings of Committee III at the 1948 Assembly, the declaration finally was adopted. The vote was forty-eight in favor, none against, two absent and eight abstentions, mostly Soviet bloc countries. The Assembly gave her a standing ovation and she wrote home, "Long job finished."

She considered the declaraction a measure of mankind's evolving ethical sense. It was not a treaty, but most international lawyers now consider it binding on states as part of the customary law of nations. Pope John XXIII in his encyclical *Pacem in Terris* described the declaration as an "important step on the path towards the juridical-political organization of the world community."

The deed validated the words: the UN could and should be used. But she wanted something more, a change in the consciences of men.

> Where, after all, do universal human rights begin? In small places, close to home—so close and so small that they cannot be seen on any maps of the world. Such are the places where every man, woman and child seeks equal justice, equal opportunity, equal dignity, without discrimination. Unless these rights have meaning there, they have little meaning anywhere.

"She was it," said a State Department official of the formulation and expression of United States policy on human rights at the UN. To a lesser degree, but perceptibly, nonetheless, she influenced United States policy and opinion in the creation of the State of Israel.

She was not a Zionist. While FDR had been alive, she accepted his view that Palestine was unable to support a larger population and in the face of Jewish homelessness and harassment examined with an open mind plans to settle the displaced Jews elsewhere than in Palestine. But facts overrode theories, especially the fact of the thousands of Jewish survivors of the Nazi extermination camps. The displaced and outcast Jews seemed propelled by an inner force Zionward only to find Palestine's gate closed by the British, who held it as a mandate. Most of the world's sympathy was with the refugees, a wave of feeling that reflected itself in the unanimity of the recommendations of an official Anglo-American Committee of Inquiry for the immediate issue of 100,000 entry certificates.

She enthusiastically embraced the committee's conclusions even as she urged the United States to take the lead and accept a share of the refugees. But the British, anxious for their ties to the Arab world, reneged on the committee's recommendations even though they had the support of the members of the commission, who had been appointed by Prime Minister Attlee. Desperate Jewish settlers organized their own defense forces and pushed an illegal immigration. The British, who had 50,000 troops in Palestine, jailed the Zionist leaders. That only strengthened the influence of the Jewish terrorists.

Eleanor was admired and respected in Britain. She knew, too, that United States cooperation and support was essential to them. She took the unusual step of sending her good friend Lady Stella Reading a letter intended for the prime minister and foreign secretary. She urged that the young Jewish terrorists seized in the wake of the bombing of British headquarters, the King David Hotel, not be executed. Great Britain's show of force had probably "built up their resistance movement since force always creates a similar attitude in the opposition." She urged the British to admit 100,000 Jews and to make a real effort to get the Arabs to agree. "Willy-nilly, the feeling grows here that it is [not] just justice which Great Britain is looking for where the Arabs are concerned, but it is that she wishes the friendship in order to get more favorable consideration where oil concessions are concerned." They were strong views, but leaders, she felt, were obligated to speak plainly. Her complaint against the politicians was that they usually lacked convictions and that the few they had they championed faintheartedly.

Her sympathy for the refugees not withstanding, as late as the end of 1946 she opposed a Jewish state, and of the many proposals at the time preferred a UN trusteeship. When a few months later the British turned the Palestine problem over to the United Nations, she hoped that was the way matters would go. But the special session of the General Assembly instead of promptly settling it established a Special Committee on Palestine (UNSCOP) to report to the regular Assembly six months later. She felt that was a cruel delay when many of the displaced had been sitting in the camps for two years waiting for a settlement of the Palestine question. A letter to Marshall decried the lack of firmness in the United States position at the special Assembly. "When we allowed the Jews to dream of a homeland and allowed many thousands of them to settle in Palestine," she wrote in "My Day," "we tactitly gave our support to this final conclusion. We are obligated today to see it through, giving every consideration, of course, to the rights of the Arabs. . . ."

The wrenching spectacle of British interception of illegal immigrant ships that were ordered back to Germany grieved her, she wrote Truman, and when he pointed to the Jewish capacity to commit outrageous acts, she replied equally firmly, "The British still seem to be on top and cruelty would seem to be on their side and not on the side of the Jews."

UNSCOP issued its report in September, just before the General Assembly opened. It recommended the end of the British mandate, and the partition of an independent Palestine into separate Jewish and Arab states, linked in an economic union, with Jerusalem as a separate entity to be administered by the UN. But the Arabs rejected any solution that recognized a Jewish homeland. As they prepared to nullify it by force, she became a vigorous advocate, within the United States delegation and government, of the partition recommendation. A struggle ensued for the minds of Truman and Marshall between the supporters of partition and the backers of the Arab cause. Her firm advocacy of partition influenced the president and secretary. Amid scenes of intense excitement, the Assembly approved partition by a vote of thirty-three (including the United States and the USSR) to thirteen, with ten nations abstaining.

The Assembly's decision transformed the problem in her mind: ". . . it would be a blow to the prestige of the United Nations from which it would never recover, if they do not implement their decision, and if we do not do our share we will be sabotaging the only machinery we have for peace today."

As Arab armies converged on Palestine, UNSCOP cautioned the UN that an international police force might be required to put partition into effect. The Defense Department and the oil people pressed hard for a change in United States policy, and the United States began to back away from the partition vote. If the UN became another League of Nations, it would make another war and a Republican victory inevitable, Eleanor warned the president. Her support of the Palestine settlers and the survivors of the holocaust was unconditional. She valued the services of her State Department advisor, Durward Sandifer, but he found her unpersuadable by the Arab case as he and other career people in the State Department saw it.

It was the United Nations that she was defending as well as the Jewish people, and she did battle with the toughest and most influential men in the government. If it required a UN police force to implement partition, she favored that. When the military opposed the proposal because it might mean a Russian contingent, she scorched the paper with her letter to the president:

"To say that just because Russia might have some soldiers in Palestine on an equal basis with us and all the other nations involved, we would have to mobilize fifty percent for war seems to me complete nonsense."

Although she was President Truman's appointee she joined several other national leaders to urge publicly the immediate establishment of a UN police force to take over in Palestine from the departing British troops.

A few months earlier she had supported a UN trusteeship for Palestine, but as Defense Secretary James Forrestal and Assistant Secretary of State Robert Lovett pressed for a retreat from partition to trusteeship, she would have none of it. Trusteeship presented the same problems of enforcement as did partition, she insisted. A moral obligation would be betrayed and the UN undermined. She was prepared to resign, she informed president and secretary: "We are evidently discarding the United Nations and acting unilaterally, or setting up a balance of power by backing the European democracies and preparing for an ultimate war between two political philosophies."

Her withdrawal from UN work would be a disaster, Truman replied immediately, and implored her not to resign. A month's trip abroad did not change her views. Adlai Stevenson asked her to come out to Illinois to help him in his quest for the governorship. She replied that she intended to stay out of the 1948 campaign:

> I am very unhappy about going back on the Assembly decision on Palestine and I feel the handling of it up to this time has brought about much of the Arab arrogance and violence. . . . Somebody will have to implement a truce [between Arabs and Jews] and somebody will have to implement a trusteeship. Some time the issue of serving on an equal basis with Russia under the United Nations will have to be faced.

Trusteeship died when the Russians opposed any shift from partition and the British said there was insufficient time for a new approach. On May 11, 1948, she cautioned Marshall that the Soviet Union was preparing to recognize the Jewish State "as soon as it is declared which will be midnight on Friday, I imagine." The president resolved to get in first. He moved so secretly that almost the entire world, including his representatives at the UN, who were still pushing trusteeship, were not informed. It came over the wires and caused "complete consternation" at the United Nations, she wrote Marshall. Her letter showed the extent to which her sympathy for the new state of Israel had attached itself to her backing of the United Nations.

> Much as I wanted the Palestine State recognized, I would not have wanted it done without the knowledge of our representatives in the United Nations who had been fighting for our changed position. I would have felt that they had to know the reason and I would also have felt that there had to be a clear understanding beforehand with such nations as we expected would follow our lead. . . . our acts which should strengthen the United Nations only result in our weakening our influence within the UN and in weakening the UN itself.

The surrounding Arab states sought to drive the Israelis into the sea. Their armies were repelled. "Henry Morgenthau brought a Mrs. Myerson [Mrs. Golda Meir] from Palestine to breakfast last Thursday. A woman of great strength and calm and for me she symbolizes the best spirit of Palestine. Evidently at last we mean to follow through on a policy of aid to the Jewish State."

There were new worries. The United States backed the peace plan of the assassinated Swedish Count Folke Bernadotte. She opposed his proposal to transfer the Negev (which the partition plan had assigned to Israel) to Jordan in return for an infertile portion of the Galilee. "I have expressed these thoughts in the delegation meetings but I do not think I carry much weight. I have only one real backer and that is Ben Cohen."

Although she minimized her influence, she carried weight, as the records of the struggle over Palestine indicate. Behind good manners and a rare ability to put herself in the other fellow's shoes was an astute negotiator on behalf of her own views. She advised Truman at the end of the 1948 General Assembly:

> The Arabs have to be handled with strength. . . . I personally feel that it is more important for the French and for the British to be united with us than for us to be united with them, and therefore when we make up our minds that something has to be done, we should be the ones to do what we think is right and we should not go through so many anxieties on the subject.

158

It was difficult to discuss the Palestine problem with Mrs. Roosevelt, complained Dr. Ralph J. Bunche, the UN official who won the Nobel Peace Prize for his successful truce negotiations after Bernadotte's assassination. She had, he thought, almost "primitive" views of the Arabs as desert-dwelling Bedouins.

Contacts with the Arabs did not change her opinion. She did not visit the Near East until February 1952 and came away with an indelible impression of Israeli dynamism and Arab passivity.

> The Arab countries are awakening but oh! So slowly and painfully! The refugees were a horror and it is the Arab governments who keep them stirred up to go home with a little help from the communists! . . .

> Israel is like a breath of fresh air after the Arab countries. Horrible problems but wonderful leaders and such able assistants. . . . I felt at home with the people of Israel.

The Jews in their own country were doing "marvels," she felt, and should, once the refugee problem was settled, help all the Arab countries.

The ability of the Arabs to accept Israeli help would take a long time, as she discovered.

14

"THERE IS NO SUCH THING AS BEING A BYSTANDER"

Part of the price of political activity in a democracy was to be criticized. She had long been inured to it, long calmly accepted the most savage and outlandlish thrusts.

"Why get into a bad smells contest?" Franklin had advised her when both were the standard subjects of columnist Westbrook Pegler's litanies of hate. He attacked Eleanor so often that he could end a speech to right-wing cohorts with the gibe, "and I haven't mentioned Eleanor Roosevelt once." No week went by without a reference to the woman he called, "The Great Gab," "La Boca Grande," "Empress Eleanor," and "The Widow." When Senator McCarthy was riding high, Pegler amiably suggested "it was time" to "snatch this wily old conspirator before Joe McCarthy's committee and chew her out." By then Pegler was writing for the Hearst press, Scripps-Howard having dropped him in 1944. And just before Mrs. Roosevelt died, the Hearst papers also let him go. She never answered him, driving him, his biographer said, into a fury.

She knew that to advocate causes that favored the dispossessed was to court trouble. She plunged on nonetheless. In 1934 Elizabeth Dilling's *Red Network* had grouped her with other suspect reformers whom the author labeled Reds and whose crime was a desire to better living conditions. The book, Eleanor wrote a correspondent in 1951, was "a tissue of lies and half-truths from beginning to end." It was, nevertheless, a bible in conservative circles. Like many others listed in that book, Eleanor had been burned in the late thirties in the rows with the Communists who up to the time of the Hitler-Stalin pact were behaving like liberals. Communist about-faces, especially those of some of her friends, had repelled her. Nevertheless, it seemed to her that much of the exposure of the Communists really reflected a hatred of Franklin and herself and a violent hope to undo the New Deal.

That had been the case with the congressional denunciations of her when, for six months, she was co-chairman of the Office of Civilian Defense. The attacks became so frenzied at that time she had felt compelled to resign. "I offered a way to get at the President," she later explained in *This I Remember.* But her broadcast just after she quit suggested she realized that she and her views were as much the target as was the president. She pointed to the "small and very vocal group of unenlightened men" who are now "able to renew, under the guise of patriotism and economy, the age-old fight of the privileged few against the good of the many."

The real intent of the attacks on her became even clearer in the South. There her advocacy of equal rights for Negroes had whipped the white supremacists into a fury. The region teemed with Eleanor stories, the most widespread being reports of "Eleanor Clubs." These were supposed to be clubs of Negro women whose alleged purpose was to get Negroes out of domestic service and white women into the kitchen. No such club ever was found, but that did not deter those who wanted to preserve Jim Crow from believing the reports.

She came away from the White House years with the deeply ingrained conviction that she was one of the targets of the witch-hunters because of her support of the underprivileged, not because the investigators thought she really was a Red. The postwar investigations did not change her mind. She viewed the various spy exposés skeptically, even after friendly newspaperwomen came up from Washington to brief her on what they were hearing. She had always disliked reactions from fear. When President Truman instituted loyalty oaths for government employees, she complied and signed one; but any Communist, she felt, would take them without scruple.

She considered the investigations as diversionary efforts by conservative groups in Congress to take the public's mind off "the very little" that Congress was doing. Alger Hiss had been one of the young State Department men who briefed her on the way to the first General Assembly. She had liked him, and when the charges against him began to surface, she had discounted them as "smears," another effort by the Right to label the New Deal as communist and foreign-inspired.

The conviction that Red-baiting was a standard tactic of the Right did not mean ignorance or naïveté about American communism. Her experience with the Communists in the thirties had left indelible marks. Because of that experience, she said half-jokingly, she was able to cope with the Russians and their allies at the UN. She preferred Americans for Democratic Action to Wallace's Progressive Citizens of America just because the former excluded Communists from leadership. Just before she went to the Geneva meeting of the Human Rights Commission at the end of 1947, one of her letters to President Truman was devoted to the matter of witch-hunts:

> It happens that I have given up any activities with the Progressive Citizens of America because I am convinced that there are people in the top levels of that organization that still are clearly connected with the Communist Party in this country or who are too chicken-hearted and afraid of being called red-baiters. Therefore, they serve the purposes of the party. . . .

But people should not be condemned because they were members of the PCA:

> I remember when my husband and I heard about a list the FBI had of organizations that were considered subversive and anyone who had contributed to these organizations was automatically considered to be questionable. My husband told me I could ask to see it and we spent an evening going through it and believe it or not, my husband's mother was one of the first people named because she had contributed to a Chinese relief organization and both Secretary Stimson and Secretary Knox were listed as having contributed to several organizations. . . .

> Forgive me for writing a long letter again but I have been troubled by what looks like a real chance that some of the methods of the Russians might be coming our way.

The hysteria that swept the country in the postwar years was her chief concern. Yet she, too, was affected by the many postwar revelations of the degree to which the communist movement had lent itself to purposes of espionage and infiltration. She became wary of the Alger Hiss case. She declined to serve as a character witness for him and in 1953 was writing correspondents, "I felt in the trial that Mr. Hiss did not tell the whole truth but I dislike so much the main witness against him that I could not bring myself to see much in that case."

Both communism and McCarthyism reflected a lack of faith in

the democratic way. "Either we are strong enough to live as a free people or we will become a police state," she wrote in "My Day." "There is no such thing as being a bystander on these questions." Senator Joseph McCarthy made his "I have in my hands" speech in Wheeling, West Virginia, in February 1950. His charge that 205 card-carrying Communists worked in the State Department was of little importance, since he never produced his list and the charge was factually untrue. Nevertheless, a large section of the public wanted to believe his charges. It wanted to believe that the setbacks to what was supposed to be an American century—represented by Russia's acquisition of the bomb, its satellization of Eastern Europe, the Communists coming to power in China—were the result of a Red conspiracy that was abetted by high officials who were "soft on Communism" rather than an inevitable dispersion and change in the distribution of power. In the face of an anti-Communist stampede, "the liberal bloc caved in," wrote an historian of the period.

Mrs. Roosevelt was not in Congress but was one of the honorable exceptions among public officials who did not retreat. She

Cardinal Spellman, she was sure, she commented in her column, had written "in what to him seems a Christian and kindly manner and I wish to do the same." She was referring to the apology he made following his public criticism of her.

counseled black leaders when they came to her with the report that they were next on the list of those to be investigated for communism. "We must fight back . . . wherever we are sure of anyone." She advised two friendly journalists that the Hearst press was going to "dissect" them. She suspected the attack might also be aimed at her— "if so I will be glad to take any part possible short of answering Pegler!"

Just before the appearance of McCarthy and McCarthyism, she had been the object of a calculated effort by the Vatican and Cardinal Spellman to drive her out of public life. Cardinal Spellman, the leading Catholic churchman in the United States, published a letter to her that ended on the peremptory note, "I shall not again publicly acknowledge you." The condign missive was triggered by her opposition to federal aid for parochial schools, but other actions had also displeased the cardinal and the Vatican. She supported birth control, had advocated Catholic participation in the American Youth Congress, opposed Catholic pressures to ban the *Nation* from school libraries, and resisted the return of ambassadors to Franco's Spain.

Despite the virulence of the cardinal's letter, her reply was unruffled—"devastating," Mayor William O'Dwyer, a leading Catholic layman, called it. She had no sense of being "an unworthy American mother," as the cardinal had charged, she wrote. "The final judgment, my dear Cardinal Spellman, of the worthiness of all human beings is in the hands of God."

She did not retreat, and public opinion rallied to her, but when Ed Flynn moved in to patch up the rift, including as part of his effort a secret visit to the Vatican, she agreed. A monsignor arrived at Hyde Park to arrange an exchange of statements. The episode ended when the cardinal on his way to dedicate a chapel in Peekskill, which was forty miles north of New York City, dropped in at Hyde Park, a further forty miles north, for a friendly chat. The amenities were preserved, but her distrust of the church as a political institution was strengthened.

She handled the cardinal's attack upon her with a composure and command that were born of a lifetime's self-discipline. Attacks upset her only when they hurt her children and her friends. When named as a correspondent by Earl Miller's wife, only upon hearing that some of her children felt their political careers were being damaged by the charges against her was she deeply upset.

Generally, she dealt with attacks by ignoring them. If people chose to believe such things about her, she said of the repeated rumors about her love affairs, there was nothing to be done. She was ready to withdraw from public life if necessary and live in the country. That readiness to retire made her a tower of strength on behalf of the things in which she believed. She had no interest in power for herself, and that freed her to be the most resolute of opponents to the demagogues and others who sought power for purposes of self-advancement.

Her standing with the public, which had always been high, became even more so. A newspaper poll in Dallas, Texas, in the fall of 1951 voted her "the greatest living American woman." At the end of that year, when the chairman of the United States delegation to the General Assembly in Paris became ill, she added the leadership of the delegation to her other duties. These also included a weekly broadcast in French to the French people. She was more than a delegate. She symbolized a great nation and reassured other nations about America's intentions. The State Department realized the impact she had on the peoples of other countries and at the end of 1951 encouraged her to visit India, Pakistan, and the Near East. She was sixty-seven. Was she able to take it physically? she asked her doctor. Reassured, she went on a visit that enhanced her own country's standing in the developing countries and America's appreciation of the needs and aspirations of the less developed.

The trip began in the Near East, where she "walked on eggs in the Arab countries because they know I believe in Israel." She went on to Pakistan. The huge masses of people who turned out to greet her elicited the comment, "I hadn't realized how they cared about Franklin." In India, the crowds, "the endless schedules, all meals official and always speeches" taxed even her boundless energy. The problems faced by the developing countries seemed "staggering," and then the sobering thought hit her: they need American help "but no one may listen after I get home."

American officials from the president down did give her a hearing. The government considered her trip a great success. She briefed committees in Congress and the Defense Department, as well as the leading officials in the CIA. Speeches and a book, *India and the Awakening East,* rounded out her effort to make the trip a useful one for the peoples whose guest she had been.

As long as she remained a member of the permanent United States mission at the United Nations, she stayed aloof from domestic politics. Any running for office was to be done by her children. Her firm views on politics and politicians were disclosed only to a few friends. She believed in the Democratic party but also felt it had been in power too long. Nevertheless, as 1952 approached, the alter-

TOP: *In Israel, February 1952, talking with Sheik Suleiman and an Israeli Army colonel. "I felt at home with the people of Israel."* BOTTOM: *In New Delhi, India, she visits Harijan colony, February 1952.*

TOP: *In New Delhi with Prime Minister Nehru and Madame Pandit.* BOTTOM: *With Golda Meir.*

native of Robert A. Taft, the isolationist Republican leader in the Senate who was the leading contender for the GOP nomination in 1951, was worse. When Dwight Eisenhower, who was the supreme commander at SHAEF, announced his candidacy early in 1952, she hoped newspaper people whom she trusted would cover him because she was genuinely interested in what he really believed. She had little doubt he would be an easy winner, if he obtained the nomination, over the Democrats who were then being mentioned, Chief Justice Vinson and Averell Harriman. As people began to talk of Adlai Stevenson, the governor of Illinois with whom she had worked at the UN, she thought he had the makings of a good president but doubted his ability to get the nomination. She liked him, but it was a distant relationship, and she kept free of preconvention maneuverings. Only when President Truman called her did she agree to come to the convention in order to speak about the UN. The standing ovation she received was marred only by the walkout of Governor Allen Shivers and part of the Texas delegation and Senator Harry F. Byrd.

She stayed out of the campaign until its very end, when, in response to Governor Stevenson's pleas, the dog-in-the-manger attitude of the regular organization, and the growing power of Senators McCarthy, William E. Jenner, and the like, she made several speeches. In Harlem her attack on Eisenhower scorched:

> I know it must have been terrible to face yourself—to realize that you have been persuaded that you must go out and stand beside men who always said things about someone who has been your best friend, someone who had really given you the opportunity to rise to great position.
>
> Yet he [Eisenhower] stood by the side of Jenner who said that General Marshall's life was a living lie.
>
> How General Eisenhower could do that I cannot understand. I cannot understand how he could give a mark of approval to Senator McCarthy.

The words must have cut deep and may have affected Eisenhower's attitude toward her. After his landslide victory, there were people in the State Department who hoped that in the American interest he would keep Mrs. Roosevelt at the UN. She doubted that, and doubted equally her ability to serve an administration that was yielding to its right wing on the issue of human rights. Her friend Baruch, a heavy contributor to the Eisenhower candidacy, told her the general had vetoed her reappointment because of remarks she was alleged to have made about Mrs. Eisenhower's drinking. But there was more to it than that. As one of J. Edgar Hoover's lieutenants reported to him after meeting with two of Eisenhower's confidants, "The General has a thorough distrust, distaste and dislike for Eleanor and told Dulles several times to get her out of the picture."

She was sad to leave her work at the UN but promptly moved across First Avenue to work with the nongovernmental organization, the American Association for the United Nations (AAUN). The Republican party was yielding to its isolationist right wing, and she believed America's relationship to the UN was again in jeopardy and required the building up of grass-roots support.

All she needed in her new job, she said, was "a cubicle." "She walked into it as if it were the Gold Room at the White House," reported A. M. Rosenthal of the *New York Times*, "and after a moment it did seem quite grand." That was the difference between Eleanor Roosevelt and most officials. The latter needed big offices, handsome desks, and large staffs to certify their importance. It worked in reverse with her. She ennobled the dingiest of places and made the people with whom she worked figures of significance. At the Paris Assembly, when she had assumed Ambassador Warren Austin's place as head of the delegation, French Sécurité had wanted to provide a guard detail as it did with other figures of prominence. She had begged off "and gotten away with it," she wrote. She did not feel she needed such an entourage for safety's sake and certainly not to enhance a sense of her importance.

At the beginning of 1953 her life was saddened by the death of Malvina Thompson, who had been with her since the late twenties. She herself had to go to the hospital for exploratory tests. They revealed nothing, her doctors said, but she realized she might soon have to slow down. She resisted doing so. She accepted the honorary chairmanship of Americans for Democratic Action. It wanted someone willing to stand up to McCarthy. The politicians were running for cover, afraid he would use their association with the liberal organization to smear them. She agreed to serve for that very reason. There were other changes in her life. She tried a new hair style. She wore stylish clothes. She reproached a fashion editor who wrote that her clothes lacked charm. Her own column went into detail about the purple and green fabric "with lights in it" that had been especially woven for her and that had provoked the writer's scorn. "I should not complain. . . . But I think every woman, no matter how old she is resents it just a little."

TOP: *In Japan, May 1953, at the Kabuki theater. "I think my being here has given the women quite a lift and has added to their sense of confidence and importance."* BOTTOM: *Sendai, Japan.*

Although Secretary of State Dulles, reflecting the attitude of the Eisenhower Administration, studiously avoided any contact with her, other countries were eager to have her visit them. So she went privately. She traveled to Japan and saw everyone from the emperor down. The most difficult moment on that trip was a visit to the city where the first A-bomb had fallen. "Hiroshima was painful," she said afterwards, but she never repudiated her support in 1945 of President Truman's decision to drop the bomb. At the end of her Japanese visit, a leading American businessman told her that she had made no mistakes and done much good for the United States.

She journeyed across half the world to Yugoslavia, a visit that included a stay with Marshal Tito on the island of Brioni. Stalin's death in the spring was followed in June by the execution of his chief policeman, Lavrenti Beria. She and Tito talked animatedly about the meaning of the changes in the Soviet leadership. One of Tito's statements impressed her particularly: "He warns against the West pushing them too hard so they can incite their people in the belief the West will attack them or their satellites."

Tito's strength as a leader interested her. Often after she returned, she speculated on what makes good leadership. Who was there, she asked, able to stand up and deal with people the way her husband, Churchill, and Stalin had. Perhaps Tito. Stevenson might after he developed more self-confidence. She suspected Truman had avoided meeting with Stalin because he lacked the confidence that he could deal with him. Eisenhower had that self-confidence, and it disappointed her that he held back and did not make imaginative use of breaks with the Soviet system like Tito's

A conflict of the thirties resounded in an exchange of letters with the president general of the Daughters of the American Revolution, who had protested Mrs. Roosevelt's reproaches that the organization backed Senator McCarthy. Its five-page, single-spaced letter noted the organization's accomplishments and its changed attitude toward Marian Anderson. Eleanor replied: ". . . I am delighted that the Daughters have come around to hold Miss Marian Anderson in high esteem but you do not remember that you refused to allow her to sing in Constitution Hall. I am delighted to hear that since then you have changed your mind."

She was certain of the organization's patriotism and love of country, her letter went on,

> but that could be said of almost all Americans and I wish you were more anxious to award prizes for plans to promote peace than for anti-aircraft gunnery.

Eleanor and her four sons in 1954. From left, John, James, Elliott, and Franklin.

I don't believe in any nation disarming alone but I heartily believe in trying to get all nations to disarm and I think you are promoting a hysteria against communism which is doing more harm than good. . . .

You are a great women's organization with a great deal of power and therefore I regret deeply that you do not use that power in being *for* things rather than against them.

She still wanted to go to Russia and planned to do so in 1954 on behalf of *Look* magazine. The United States Embassy in Moscow did not ask her to stay there. "The Bohlens may be afraid to have me," she explained. In the end she canceled the trip when the Russians vacillated about giving a visa to any of the people she wanted to bring.

"No, I have not slackened my pace," she told Emma Bugbee of

the *Herald-Tribune* on the eve of her seventieth birthday. "At least, not yet. I probably shall. Everybody does."

She allowed the AAUN to celebrate her birthday so that it might raise funds to pay off the organization's debts. Her faith in the UN had not faltered, she told the audience of UN and United States notables (minus any representative of the Eisenhower Administration):

> As for accomplishments, I just did what I had to do as things came along. I got the most satisfaction from my work in the UN. There I was part of the second great experiment to bring countries together and to get them to work for a peaceful atmosphere in the world, and I still feel it important to strengthen this organization in every way.

Asked about the way she viewed life, she replied: "Life has got to be lived—that's all there is to it. At seventy, I would say the advantage is that you take life more calmly. You know that 'this, too, shall pass.'"

"OF COURSE I KNOW — IT'S MRS. ROOSEVELT"

"Of course I know—it's Mrs. Roosevelt." This cartoon, by Herbert Block, was for the American Association for the United Nations dinner given in celebration of her seventieth birthday.

173

15

CAMPAIGN FOR THE DEMOCRATIC SOUL

A s usually happens with people as they grow older, life's time-
table seemed to accelerate. In 1955 the theatrical producer and bon
vivant John Golden, a friend with whom she lunched weekly at Sar-
di's, died. "After 40 we all live on borrowed time," she wrote her
daughter. "Just a few more holes in this life to warn us to be prepared." She had always fought off the sense of being a stranger in
life by keeping busy. And the way to keep from feeling old, she now
sternly told herself, was to keep being useful. "Unless time is good
for something, it is good for nothing," she wrote.

Freed of official responsibilities, she traveled more widely than
before. She made the trips more congenial by having friends along,
usually Maureen Corr, her Irish-born secretary who had succeeded
Tommy; children and grandchildren; Trude Lash; and especially
David. He was part of her daily thought and deep in her heart.

In 1955 she went to Israel with Trude and Maureen. That gave
her a chance to stop over in Paris and London. In the United States,
a Republican administration had orders to stay away from her.
Abroad, leaders both in government and out were eager to see her
and exchange the bits of information that gave each greater authority. In the summer of 1955 she went to Japan for a second look and
then went on to Indonesia via Hong Kong and Manila. She was
especially eager to learn how people who lived next to Red China
judged it. America's policy of reconquest of the mainland and nonrecognition made little sense to her. In Indonesia she ended up on
Bali, where she saw "enough dancing to last me the rest of my life."
In Bangkok she attended sessions of the World Federation of United

Visiting a camp in France for Jewish children, en route to Israel from Morocco, March 13, 1955.

Nations Association and visited Angkor Wat. She had learned to be interested in anything that came her way, but she also made special efforts to experience all that she could as deeply as she could.

An increasing fondness for Adlai Stevenson added zest to these years. She was sure after the 1952 campaign that she wanted to do whatever possible to get him another chance at the presidency. Anything that the Stevenson people asked of her she did. She campaigned in the primaries, helped raise funds, buoyed up his spirits when they flagged. As 1956 approached, she was "running around madly" for him.

Part of her service to him was to help the Democratic national chairman draft a civil rights plank for the convention that was accepted by the black leaders yet kept the South within the party. Averell Harriman, Stevenson's chief rival for the nomination, sought to paint

175

Campaign for the presidency. Eleanor with (from left) Senator H. Lehman, Adlai Stevenson, and New York City Mayor Robert Wagner. "I have never worked as I have this autumn in our national campaign."

the Illinoisan as the candidate of "moderation," a word that black leaders read to mean passivity. The Supreme Court in the *Brown* decision in 1954 had banned segregation in the schools by striking down "the separate but equal" doctrine. Would the Democrats "support," "approve," or "endorse" the ruling? Would they seek to enforce the ruling by urging action in Congress to deny federal aid to segregated schools? Blacks had voted strongly for Stevenson in 1952, and Harriman hoped to take away this support by underscoring Stevenson's "moderation" on these issues.

Stevenson's problem was to keep the South Democratic without losing the support of the northern cities. It would have been difficult to do without the support of Eleanor Roosevelt, whom Stevenson considered "the voice most respected among Negroes." She wrote him in June: "Somehow I think understanding and sympathy for the white people in the South is as important as understanding and support and sympathy for the colored people. We don't want another war between the states and so the only possible solution is to get the leaders of both sides together and try to work first steps out."

This was a strange role for the woman who had always been in the forefront of the struggle for Negro rights. Afterwards she was not sure she had been right. But her goal was to get Stevenson elected, and she had seen enough of Franklin's and Louis's operations to know one often had to balance objectives in politics. She was sure that Stevenson, if elected, would be right on the issues and threatened at one point to withdraw from the board of directors of the NAACP because its executive director had suggested blacks might not support Stevenson's candidacy. But her absoluteness of commitment to Stevenson obscured the urgency of the civil rights issue. The Supreme Court school desegregation ruling had doomed segregation in law; it was still the rule in practice. Moderation turned out to be one of the code words for its continuance. Among white leaders she would be in the forefront of the fight to end discrimination, but its essential driving force would come from the nonviolent resistance movement led by Dr. Martin Luther King in the sixties.

"I know I should live more reasonably," she told friends in the midst of the preconvention campaign, "but I can't till after November 6th." She arrived in Chicago for the convention and promptly Stevenson's managers whisked her off to a press conference, where they hoped she might undo the damage of Harry S. Truman's announcement the day before for Harriman. In forty-five minutes of give-and-take she effectively deflated the Truman drive. Truman had said Stevenson lacked the experience to be president. He was as well equipped, she remarked, as Truman had been when he became president in 1945, and he was better equipped than Harriman in foreign affairs. She refused to take seriously Truman's characterization of Harriman as the "fighting" candidate when Stevenson had fought it out in the primaries while Harriman had avoided them. As for the charge of moderation, she felt the southern members of the platform committee had come a long way. She and Truman were getting old, she reminded the press, and it was time for both of them to yield to younger leaders in the party.

"It was an adroit and ruthless performance," Arthur Schlesinger, Jr., one of Stevenson's top aides, said admiringly. Awed columnists commented that no other northerner could have survived politically after saying the things she did.

Stevenson was nominated, and that had been her topmost purpose in coming to Chicago. She also addressed the convention. Her impassioned plea to the Democrats to go beyond the New Deal and Fair Deal and embark on a campaign to end poverty in America moved Edward R. Murrow, a seasoned political observer, to call it "the greatest convention speech I ever heard." New problems must be met in new ways, she emphasized. "Our party may be the oldest democratic party, but our party must live on as a young party, and it must have young leadership." She recalled FDR's pledge to better the conditions of the one-third of a nation that was ill-housed, ill-clothed, and ill-fed. Twenty percent was the figure in 1956. "Could we have the vision of doing away in this country with poverty?"

The effort to give the Democratic party a new vision in the context of history transcended the importance of her struggle for Adlai. It was extraordinary that someone who second only to FDR personified the New Deal should have sounded the call for new solutions to fit the circumstances.

Characteristically, she thought she had done poorly and hurried off from Chicago to spend a month in Europe with two grandsons and Grania Gurewitsch, David's daughter. She showed them her favorite places—museums, restaurants, streets—and met friends.

No sooner was she back in September than she appeared on "Meet The Press" to give what Stevenson called "the wisest, most gracious and convincing performance in my recollection." He promptly sent a memo to his campaign manager to schedule him for some joint appearances with her and to try to place her on one of the large nationwide hookups: "I am told that her Meet The Press performance was masterful—especially her characterization of Ike as a man whose experience lay in carrying out policies, not in formulating them, and her reminder that Nixon had called [Representative] Helen Gahagan Douglas a communist although he knew it was untrue."

She never had worked as hard as she did in the 1956 campaign, she said after an autumn of schedules as grueling almost as Stevenson's own. The Democrats did win the Senate and the House, but Eisenhower was reelected in a landslide. "No one could have done more," she consoled the defeated candidate, "but the love affair between President Eisenhower and the American people is too acute at the present time for any changes to occur."

Never one to brood over a political defeat, she promptly resorted to her usual recipe of work and helpfulness to get over it. She took a trip to Morocco, combining a holiday with aid to the Moroccan Jews, an old community that was being forced to emigrate. She began work on a new book, *On My Own.* The Scripps-Howard chain's failure to renew her contract for "My Day" was a blow. She did not wish to preach mainly to the converted but was glad to get another New York outlet in the New York *Post.*

Although she was proud of her column, her monthly question-and-answer page in *McCalls,* and her books, she never thought of herself as having "style" as a writer. Even as good a friend as Hick lamented her failure to go about the business of writing more professionally and urged her not to dash off her column in an hour, as she was wont to do. Some of her draft chapters, Bruce Gould of the *Ladies' Home Journal* had once complained, read as if they had been composed riding on a bicycle. She had plenty to say, and her judgments, crisp and straightforward, reflected a flawless taste and a morality rooted in love. She was too busy living to take more time to write, yet there was scarcely a column or letter that did not approach the aphoristic.

In 1957 the publisher of the *Post,* Dorothy Schiff, asked her to go to Red China and the Soviet Union for the paper. She wanted to do so. Dulles turned down her request to travel in China, but the Russians were eager to have her come. In September 1957 she arrived in Moscow with David and Maureen. They traveled widely through the country, to Tashkent and Samarkand and the Black Sea as well as to Moscow and Leningrad. The life of the people was improving, she concluded, but politics remained the monopoly of a handful. Just before her departure for home Nikita Khrushchev, the premier, sent word from the Crimea, where he was on holiday in his dacha, that he would see her. The next day she was in Yalta, visited the site of the Big Three conference and then arrived at Khrushchev's. A short, stocky, ebullient man, he met her in a Russian peasant's blouse. They went at it for several hours, agreeing in the end that they had disagreed. The Russian visit gave her the final chapters for *On My Own.* They contained the conclusion that she would die if she had to live in Soviet Russia.

In 1958 David Gurewitsch remarried, and she had the wedding in her apartment. When she returned to Russia in 1958, David and his wife Edna accompanied her. The visit included attendance at the sessions of the World Federation of United Nations Associations. She took the time to write Anna her views on dealing with the Russians:

> It is difficult to assess the value of contact unless you accept the need for our recognition of realities. If we accept Mr. Dulles['s] theory that men want to be free so communism can't last, then there is no value in what we did as a delegation or are now doing as individuals. If, however, we believe that communism is here to stay awhile and that we must live together and very slowly changes may be coming in both our systems which will make co-existence possible, then I think intercourse has value. Now, we talk, but we don't mean the same things and we dare not try to clarify unless we manage to talk alone with one individual. We need some realistic re-thinking in high places I think about the U.S.S.R. and China.

She knew it was her last trip to Russia—"my time is limited and I should see new things or stay at home." She was delighted on her return to plan sharing a house with David and Edna. It would take

With Maureen Corr in Russia, 1957.

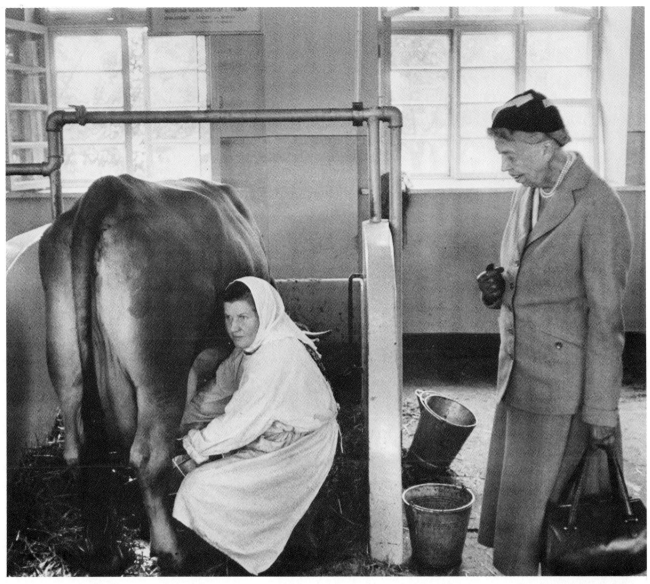

A cooperative farm near Tashkent.

some time before her two-floor apartment would be ready, but she looked foward to moving in and to a relationship that helped her ward off loneliness in her final years.

A new note sounded in her political utterances in 1959. She had become convinced Stevenson was unable to get across to people and doubted his electability as president. Whoever was the Democratic candidate in 1960, however, should make him secretary of state if he won.

A granddaughter, Nina, accompanied her that year to Israel and Iran. Anna and James Halsted were spending a year in the latter country, and she wanted to visit them. She had rarely felt so isolated from the news as there. Before she left she lunched with the shah, "nice but dull," she decided. In Israel she found "the dream

With Israeli Prime Minister David Ben-Gurion. "I think Israel will survive because of her leaders," she wrote after her 1959 visit.

of building a country" still alive and still everywhere. The country was lucky to have in David Ben-Gurion a leader who knew how to capture the imagination of the young. Always she was appraising, estimating from the point of view of a leader, and when a man or woman turned out to have the qualities of self-command and command, her spirits soared.

The Democratic Advisory Committee celebrated her seventy-fifth birthday. It was a relpay of the 1956 convention tussle between herself and former President Truman for the soul of the Democratic party. On this occasion the struggle was over the role of "liberals" in the Democratic party. He would not bar them but would subordinate them to the practical politicians, Truman said. He was not against them but wanted working, not talking, liberals. It was Eleanor's turn to speak. Tall, stately, and patrician, she demurred. She had immediately sensed Truman's real target were the Stevenson loyalists, especially those who declined to defer to the practical politicians who were dead set against a third Stevenson try in 1960. The president did not like certain kinds of liberalism.

"I welcome every kind of liberal that begins to learn by coming into our party what it is to work on being a liberal," she said. She and Truman now were seventy-five, she noted, and added, older people "have something to learn from liberals that are younger." She believed in the Democratic party, her speech ended, and the sentiments that followed were similar to ones she had used with Franklin time and again: "I want unity, but above everything else, I want a party that will fight for the things that we know to be right at home and abroad."

16

MEETING LIFE
WITH
ADVENTUROUS
COURAGE

I SUPPOSE I should slow down," she told reporters in 1961 on her seventy-seventh birthday, and then in several pithy sentences expounded a philosophy of living that had turned the woman who in 1942 said "It is a terrible thing to know me" into a model of how to cope with life's absurdities as well as satisfactions.

"I think I have a good deal of my Uncle Theodore in me, because I could not, at any age, be content to take my place in a corner by the fireside and simply look on."

"Life must be lived. Curiosity must be kept alive."

"The fatal thing is the rejection. One must never, for whatever reason, turn his back on life."

"The thing I am most grateful for," she said in another interview, "is for an interesting life—and the opportunities I had to learn along the way."

In 1960 the specialists who had been brought in by David Gurewitsch diagnosed her fevers as aplastic anemia. The year before she had talked with David Lilienthal "about not getting too self-absorbed" when the disorders of age began to invade the body. "Inevitably there are aches and pains, more and more, and if you pay much attention to them, the first thing you know you're an invalid."

So she began the final years of life. She then was sharing a house with David and Edna. She continued to lecture, became a professor at Brandeis, did a television series called "The Prospects of Mankind" produced by Henry Morgenthau, the son of the former secretary. "My Day" appeared now only three times a week but was printed in forty-six papers, her syndicate told her. She remained ready for new experiences. ". . . [W]hen you cease to make a contribution you begin to die," she wrote a correspondent. "Therefore, I think it a necessity to be doing something which you feel is helpful in order to grow old gracefully and contentedly."

Behind her kindliness and old-fashioned courtesy, the one-time ugly duckling had grown into a giant killer. Since Franklin's death, the tall lady in a flowered hat had wrested a charter of human rights from the jumble of interests that constituted the United Nations, bested Vishinsky on the issue of forced repatriation of refugees, and made man, not the nation-state, the new measure of all things. She had withstood Cardinal Spellman, the powerful head of the American hierarchy. She was Stevenson's chief campaigner in his bids for the presidency and in 1961, allied with Herbert Lehman, Robert Wagner, and other reformers, had put an end to Carmine De Sapio, the boss of Tammany. The do-gooder was now recognized as an astute and tough old bird. She emerged, said a commentator, "as one of the great women in a history where women have seldom been allowed their political head."

Her political strength lay in the fact that she never wanted power for herself but only for the good it might achieve. For a few months

"I am not a candidate," Stevenson insisted in 1960, but Mrs. Roosevelt would not take no for an answer.

With, right, Lyndon B. Johnson and Anthony B. Ackers, chairman of Citizens for Kennedy in the 1960 presidential campaign. She supported John Kennedy reluctantly at first but altered her position when he became the nominee. Later, she took on many assignments for him as president.

in 1960 she held back from the race for the Democratic presidential nomination. But, troubled then by the specter of Joseph Kennedy that loomed behind a son whose flirtation with Joe McCarthy she did not forget, and whose ties with the Catholic Church made her uneasy, she became a major strategist in the effort of Stevenson loyalists to draft him for another try.

She did in Los Angeles much of what she had done for Stevenson in Chicago in 1956. In a white cotton dress with a V-neck, slightly stooped, a shuffle replacing the wonted springlike stride, she addressed caucuses, spoke to the convention, held a press conference in support of a Stevenson-Kennedy ticket. The old fluted voice held forth. The delegates listened respectfully, almost reverentially, to the "fine, precise, hard-worked like ivory" figure, in Norman Mailer's words, but she did not stop Kennedy's first-ballot steamroller.

She hurried off from the convention without speaking with its nominee, irritated with herself. Three of her sons had supported Kennedy, and she did not like to be in opposition to them. She was afraid her fight for Stevenson had embarrassed him and weakened his chances of being named secretary of state if Kennedy were elected. Publicly she accepted defeat graciously: ". . . I really enjoy a good fight, and those of us who fought for Stevenson fought a good fight." Privately she withheld active support for the nominee until the two met at Hyde Park and she was assured that he intended to make the best possible use of men like Stevenson and Chester Bowles. Kennedy came away from his meeting "absolutely smitten with this woman," according to William Walton, his New York coordinator, who accompanied him.

She agreed to do whatever he wanted in the campaign. She spoke in New York, which was one of the decisive states. She praised him in her column. She proffered advice—through Franklin Jr. and by letter—cautioning him on his declared policy toward Cuba and warning him against "last minute" tricks by Richard Nixon.

A few months later she attended Kennedy's inaugural, sitting in the stands below. She arrived early and wrapped herself in an army blanket as well as a mink coat to guard against the brilliant day's twenty-degree temperature. She had refused to sit with the new president's party on the platform but left Washington buoyed by hoped in the younger generation led by the new president.

She did innumerable chores for him. She counseled him to train his voice so that he might find a forum similar to Franklin's fireside chats. When the Bay of Pigs turned into humiliation and disaster,

187

she joined a Tractors for Freedom Committee to negotiate with Castro for an exchange of prisoners. She served on the National Advisory Council of the Peace Corps. She pressed the president and Stevenson, his ambassador at the UN, to appoint more women to policy-making posts. She submitted lists of "really able women" to both men and agreed afterward to chair the president's Commission on the Status of Women. Law, custom, and men's forgetfulness, she said, were keeping women from equal opportunities in government and other jobs.

She insisted stoutly that she was not a feminist. "I do not think women should be judged as women alone when it comes to appointing them or electing them purely because they are women. I should always judge a candidate, whether a man or woman, on fitness for office. I would like to see us get away from considering a man or woman from the point of view of religion, color or sex."

A few months before she died she was again asked her position on the Equal Rights Amendment. Her views had altered. Just before the 1944 Democratic National Convention she had exchanged memos with Franklin in which both had indicated it might be time to drop their opposition.

Memorandum for the President:
    I am getting information from those who have been opposed [to the amendment] in the past. May be time to change.

The White House
E.R.
February 9, 1944

Memorandum for
MRS. ROOSEVELT
    In regard to the Equal Rights Amendment, I have always been for it in principle but have felt that a Constitutional Amendment might make it more difficult to prevent the enactment of certain necessary safeguards for women.

    Frankly, I am not as much worried about the proposed amendment as I used to be. I am inclined to think the safeguards could always be enacted with or without the amendment.

    In other words, I do not think it is a vital necessity in the next Platform but if it is put in I will not weep about it!

F.D.R.

The Democrats did endorse it in 1944, but she was unable to get herself to do more than tepidly approve it as she did in 1951. When again queried about it in May 1962 at the Overseas Press Club, she replied, "Many of us opposed the amendment because we felt it would do away with protection in the labor field. Now with unionization, there is no reason why you shouldn't have it if you want it."

That was the best she could do. She had long battled for women's rights but saw them as subordinate to social reform. She refused to view social problems "through the unique lens of gender."

Peace and the United Nations remained dominating concerns. Soon after Kennedy assumed office, she wrote him that she had just signed a "Declaration of Conscience and Responsibility" circulated by the Quakers. Her follow-up letter urged a withdrawal of troops on both sides of the dividing line in middle Europe and demilitarization of the area. She understood that not having German troops meant a weakening of NATO, but if the Russians made equal concessions, that was a good way to begin disarmament. "There will have to be some give and take," but she was worried that "in the present frame of mind of most of the country any kind of giving will be appeasement."

She joined other members of the AAUN to go to Washington to urge the government to take the Vietnam issue to the UN. They were rebuffed. Another prescient position was to urge the president to seek an agreement with the Russians to keep outer space demilitarized. "I perfectly understand the pressures that the Pentagon and probably some of the scientists are bringing on you, but I do feel that such action on our part is really a challenge to the Russians to feel complete freedom to do anything they desire in this area. Perhaps you would be glad of a little opposition."

"On so many issues," an observer later wrote, "she saw further because she felt deeper."

In October 1960, in the midst of the Kennedy-Nixon presidential race, Nikita Khrushchev and other world leaders had come to the General Assembly, where Khrushchev had unloosed a violent attack, including a banging of a shoe on his desk, against Dag Hammarskjold. She was outraged. It was not differences in economic systems, as Khrushchev contended, that caused the real difficulty between communist and noncommunist countries, she wrote in her column. "The difficulty really lies in the different concept of the meaning of individual freedom, of individual participation and responsibility in government." The West was concerned "with the basic freedoms of human beings," whereas Khrushchev as she watched him made it easy to see "he is not accustomed to listening to opposing points of views and giving them due respect." "One of the best you've ever written," her syndicate wrote her.

In the midst of Khrushchev's rowdy performance, which in retrospect can be seen as aimed more at Red China than Hammarskjold, she invited the Russian premier to tea. To critics for having done so, she answered, "We have to face the fact that either all of us are going to die together or are going to learn to live together and if we are to live together we have to talk."

In early 1962 she was puzzled by ardent messages she received from Nikita Khrushchev and his wife on the occasion of FDR's eightieth birthday. Khrushchev's cable endorsed Roosevelt's belief that ideological differences should not impede "businesslike cooperation." She showed the messages to Adlai and on his suggestion sent them on to Secretary of State Rusk, noting, "I am as bewildered as possible by this sudden influx of goodwill. If you have any explanation I would be grateful if you would let me know." Afterward she wrote Khrushchev guardedly that she appreciated his "kind words" and would be heartened if relations between Russia and the United

The Khrushchevs at Hyde Park in September 1959. Behind Mrs. Khrushchev is Andrei Gromyko. "We have to face the fact that either all of us are going to die together or we are going to live together and if we are going to live together we have to talk."

190

States "could become more realistic and more cooperative. This must largely come about under the aegis of the United Nations."

Stevenson asked her to serve as a delegate to the Assembly in the spring of 1961. She accepted, but an attack of the "flu," really phlebitis, sidelined her. She did drop in as a guest at a meeting of the eighteen-nation Human Rights Commission, where the United States was represented by Marietta P. Tree. The commission's chairman, Chandra S. Jha of India, asked her to speak. She hoped to see the day when the principles enunciated in the declaration would be accepted as law. "Then we will have made real steps forward in human rights." She had been of "very little use" to Stevenson, she wrote him after the special Assembly, and when he asked whether he might list her as "Special Advisor" to the regular session, she agreed, on his assurance that "the duties would be within your discretion."

Early the following year she was told by Abba Schwartz, one of the people who served as a liaison with the president and now an assistant secretary of state, that the president had nominated her for a Nobel prize. "I must frankly tell you," she wrote the president, "that I cannot see the faintest reason why I should be considered."

Although she was slowing down, she championed the cause of black equality wherever she had a chance. When Dr. Martin Luther King's "freedom marchers" were jailed in Albany, Georgia, she wrote the attorney-general, Robert Kennedy, on their behalf. A settlement

". . . I think I accomplished what Adlai wanted in just appearing at the UN," she wrote President Kennedy after the special session of the General Assembly.

TOP: *Christmas Day dinner at Val-Kill, 1959. Mrs. Roosevelt's grandson Curtis is pouring the wine.* BOTTOM: *In the woods at Val-Kill, 1956.*

TOP: *At Val-Kill with two of John Roosevelt's daughters, Sally (at her side) and Nina (in the boat). Fala is on the leash and Tamas is the other Scotty.* BOTTOM: *Four generations: Mrs. Roosevelt, Anna on the left, granddaughter "Sistie" (Mrs. Seagrave) on the right, and great-granddaughter Eleanor in Mrs. Seagrave's arms.*

had been reached, he replied. "You are doing very well and the results are gratifying," she came back. Among her last acts was to invite Dr. King to be the first guest on her new television program. Even more telling of her attitude toward blacks was an episode in Greenwich Village. A station wagon backed into her in the rain and knocked her down. The driver was a black youth, and her first thought was to tell him to get away quickly; she hobbled off with her torn ligaments to her speaking engagement.

"The essence of discrimination, or segregation, is that it enables those who practice it to avoid reality," said Robert C. Weaver, the administrator of the Housing and Home Finance Administration and a black. "Mrs. Roosevelt, however, knew Negroes, was seen in public with Negroes, entertained Negroes in her home, and was entertained by Negroes in their homes. By doing so she not only demolished social barriers—barriers that were much more rigid thirty years ago than they are today—but she made people ashamed that those barriers existed. . . . A great deal of the progress Negroes have made since 1932 in emerging from the darkness into which they were thrust after Reconstruction came through the efforts of Mrs. Roosevelt."

A melancholy measure of waning strength was a resigned letter to each of her children after a particularly heated session at Hyde Park. She refused to assess blame but told them:

> One has to work for whatever one really wants in this world. Such conditions don't just grow, much thought and many acts of unselfish devotion are required day by day, but without it family ties deteriorate and are weakened, and the nation suffers.
>
> I think this responsibility is hard for the next generation to face when one member of the older generation lives on beyond the allotted span. I have determined therefore to hold no more "reunions". . . . I love you all very much and I am proud of you when you are your best selves. . . . You can however make me unhappy and it affects me more deeply when things go wrong among you than when it touches the relationship with me. You are, I hope going to live and work together for many years to come, my time, I hope is limited . . .
>
> Mother

She stuggled against succumbing to her illness but in the summer of 1962 was ordered by the doctors to the hospital for a blood transfusion. She was scheduled to go to Campobello for the opening of a bridge that linked the island to the mainland. She wrote the president that if he and others in his administration came, she hoped they would come to a buffet luncheon at the Campobello house.

The president could not come, but she did get to the "beloved island," as Franklin's parents had dubbed Campobello. The first column she filed from there was titled "The Patient Survived." She told of having gone to the hospital for tests. Finally the doctor said, "I'm finished. Good night." The patient sank back into her pillows wanting nothing more than to be left alone, she wrote. An intern came. "Sorry to bother you, but what were your mother and father's names?" "This was a night in the hospital," her column went on. When she had suggested it was not exactly restful, "they looked at her in a mild surprise. 'What do we have laboratories for?' they said. 'This is why we want you in the hospital.' "

"Eureka, they have you there! You get well, but is it worth it?"

She drove down from Campobello, stopping in Boston to see young Henry Morgenthau and his wife Ruth. Earlier she had sent Henry, as she did regularly, flowers in remembrance of his mother's birthday. "I am on the way to recovery," she wrote, stretching the truth a little. She stopped for a short visit with Esther on the way to Hyde Park. The Walter Reuthers were in Hyde Park over Labor Day weekend, and talking with him acted as a tonic. But the next morning she was scarcely able to raise a teacup to her mouth. Though she was running a fever, she insisted on working with Ruth Denniston on her last book, *Tomorrow Is Now*. She finally had to allow her to leave earlier than she had planned.

The final sad weeks began. Trude Lash wrote in a letter to Paul Tillich:

> She was not afraid of death at all. She welcomed it. She was so weary and so infinitely exhausted, it seemed as though she had to suffer every human indignity, every weakness, every failure that she had resisted and conquered so daringly during her whole life—as though she were being punished for being too strong and powerful and disciplined and almost immune to human frailty.

She died on November 7, 1962.

She did not know whether she believed there was a future life, she had told Edward R. Murrow. But there must be "some reason" for "all that you go through here." Whether there was or wasn't, she

TOP: *Mrs. Roosevelt is buried in the Rose Garden at Hyde Park. From left, Mrs. Lyndon B. Johnson, Mrs. John F. Kennedy, President Kennedy, Vice President Johnson, former President Harry S. Truman, Mrs. Truman, and former president Dwight D. Eisenhower.* BOTTOM: *The "It's Her" cartoon appeared in the* St. Louis Post Dispatch *November 13, 1962.*

"IT'S HER."

finally decided it had to be faced "in exactly the same way"—that is, the important thing was that you never let down doing the best that

you were able to do—it might be poor because you might not have much within you to give, or to help other people with, or to live your life with. But as long as you did the very best that you were able to do, then that was what you were put here to do and that was what you were accomplishing by being here.

And so I have tried to follow that out—and not to worry about the future or what was going to happen. I think I am pretty much of a fatalist. You have to accept whatever comes and the only important thing is that you meet it with courage and with the best that you have to give.

Few women in American history had posed to themselves more steadily questions like "what am I here for, what is life's purpose, who am I?" The spirit that had prompted such questioning had infused the Roosevelt years. The American Great Seal contains an open eye within a radiant nimbus at the tip of a pyramid above which is the inscription *annuit coeptis*—"he smiles at our undertaking." Her gaze reflected that eye.

"While she was with us," wrote Doris Fleeson, columnist and old friend, "no man had to feel entirely alone."

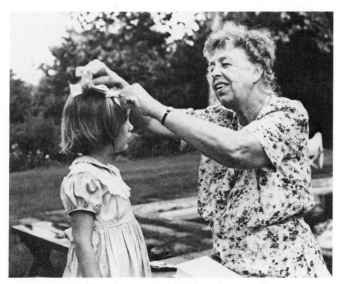

With John Roosevelt's daughter Sally
at Hyde Park, August 1951.

Val-Kill, 1962.

B   c.2 B
Roosevelt
        Lash. Joseph P.
        Life was meant to be
lived.